DON'T TAKE THAT JOB

'TIL YOU READ THIS BOOK

9 Lenses to Look Through Before You Leap

Leigh Branham and Mark Hirschfeld

ACKNOWLEDGEMENTS

Leigh would like to thank his mentor, Richard Nelson Bolles, author of **What Color is Your Parachute?,** whose influence on the way millions of people around the world seek and find fulfilling work has been immeasurable.

Mark would like to thank his wife Nancy and children, Jillian and Jacob, who are his inspiration. Thanks to Sami Foust, who designed our cover. Thanks to Debbie Manning, who asked for help to support folks who had been furloughed or lost their job in the pandemic—her request sparked this work!

Thanks to our panel of esteemed experts, whose clear, no-nonsense guidance is a cornerstone of this book. Grateful to all the folks we've had the opportunity to come along side and help in their job search and career journeys. You have been our teachers, and this book is better because of you.

Contents

Introduction

If you have learned from your experience, prepared yourself for this moment, and have a good attitude, you deserve a great job in a great workplace.

But...maybe you feel you can't be picky. Maybe you needed a job yesterday to pay your bills and you can't afford the luxury of pausing to consider whether it's the best possible fit for you. We get it. That is a dilemma that millions face every day. Of course, no job is perfect, and we cannot know everything there is to know before accepting a job. There will always be unpleasant surprises (and sometimes even pleasant ones).

Still, there is much you can do to minimize the unpleasant surprises before you join a prospective employer that will keep you from making a serious career misstep. That is a major part of our mission in writing this book. Many job seekers feel so lucky and excited to have a job offer that it never occurs to them that they should have researched the prospective employer and asked a few well-chosen questions during their pre-hire interviews. Others know they should ask questions in the interview, but may not know what to ask, or they may be afraid that asking too many questions would be off-putting to the interviewer. To show enthusiasm while also casting a skeptical eye is a delicate balance.

Nick's Story

Just six months into his new job, Nick resigned. He had been promised extensive training to bring him up to speed, but never received it. He struggled to keep up with the pace of activity and the chaos caused by his manager's failure to plan. When Nick asked for one-on-one time with his manager to go over a complex project, the manager never had time for him.

Nick had sensed his manager didn't really know enough to be able to thoroughly brief him anyway. When he had given Nick feedback about work that was unacceptable, he wasn't specific about how to correct it. He seemed to enjoy intimidating people and he had a terrible temper. He would ask a question and if Nick didn't know the answer, he would make fun of him in front of coworkers.

Months later, when Nick had mastered every needed skill required for the next higher level, the manager bluntly denied Nick the promotion he had promised. As time passed, Nick's suspicion was born out--that his manager's behavior was generally tolerated throughout the company, all the way up to the senior-executive level. Nick turned in his resignation and was reemployed at another company within two months. He now reports to a manager he loves.

Nick's story illustrates how a series of progressive triggering events can lead any employee to gradually disengage and then suddenly quit a job. Looking back, you wonder what Nick could have done to learn about the organization's management culture before accepting the job in the first place.

Part of our mission is to help those, like Nick in the example above, who are already employed but are feeling bored, restless, stuck, miserable, or just plain tired of "sucking it up." If this describes your current situation and you are ready to make a change, the following chapters will provide you with a systematic process of self-reflection and action that will help you move forward in your career.

If you are struggling with the decision about whether to stay or go, you will benefit from our guidelines to consider before you quit, which appear later in this introduction. You will also find tips, insights, and advice from our esteemed panel of twenty experts that will help you decide. You may realize that your best option is to have a necessary conversation with your manager to resolve an issue. Or you may create a new job or role for yourself by uncovering a hidden need in the organization that requires your talent to fill.

The Lenses: Based on the Reasons Employees Leave

Leigh's earlier book, *The 7 Hidden Reasons Employees Leave: How to Recognize the Subtle Signs and Act Before It's Too Late,* was based on his careful analysis of 21,000+ third-party, post-exit interviews with departed employees at all levels from companies in 17 different industries and his careful reading of their rich verbatim comments.

The reasons those employees voluntarily left their employers were mainly due to one or more of the following dissatisfactions:

1. The job or workplace was not as expected
2. The mismatch between job and person
3. Too little coaching and feedback
4. Too few growth and advancement opportunities
5. Feeling devalued and unrecognized
6. Stress from overwork and work-life imbalance
7. Loss of trust and confidence in senior leaders

These seven reasons are unsurprising to most at first glance, but they are hidden in one important sense--most managers believe the main reason workers leave is "more pay." It's not surprising that most managers believe that because most departing employees do receive pay increases and are happy to say so during their exit interviews. But "more pay" or "better opportunity "may only scratch the surface of more complex motivations and circumstances. The "pull-factor" reasons--pay and opportunity--often obscure and fail to capture the true root-cause dissatisfaction that caused the departing employee to start thinking about leaving in the first place.

Most people don't want to burn a bridge when they leave a job, so they often just give the answer of what "pulled" them out instead of what "pushed" them out, especially when speaking directly to a manager whose way of managing may be the very reason they chose to quit. The root cause of turnover is usually more likely to be found in the "push" factor.

Having been career transition and job search coaches for much of our careers, we were not surprised that pay, though important to us all, is not the simple reason for most voluntary exits. Nor were we surprised by the depth of frustration, anger, and disappointment that departing employees often express.

But their plaintive comments serve as a reminder of how little research so many job seekers do before they accept an offer. Why is this so? For many, their financial situation dictates an urgency that makes it hard to "be picky." We can be so desperate to find <u>A</u> job that the idea of finding <u>THE</u> job with the right employer seems unrealistic and a luxury we cannot afford to pursue.

As one job seeker commented on Reddit, "I don't want 'A job' I want a job with a good company...which is incredibly rare nowadays."

Further Evidence: Based on 2.1 million Surveys

Our book, *Re-Engage: How America's Best Workplaces Inspire Extra Effort in Extraordinary Times* (based on 2.1 million employee surveys from 10,000 employers in *Best-Place-To-Work* competitions in 44 cities) documented that the better places to work are the exceptions, not the rule.

If you are looking for the right job in a better workplace, this book is for you.

You may not be sure what job you want. You may be actively job-seeking and preparing for one or more job interviews. You may even be expecting a job offer or already negotiating one. You may suspect employer bias is working against you. Or, like many who go uncounted in the monthly unemployment numbers, you may have given up looking for a job entirely.

The pandemic of 2020-2022 upended the lives of many workers, but also gave them time to think--a chance to reassess what they want and need from their work. Many of those who were given the opportunity to work from home (or just about anywhere) are now reluctant to go back into the office. They now find that remote work options are more available at more workplaces. This has created more choice about where to work while staff shortages gave many more leverage with both current and prospective employers. Many employers have raised workers' pay to stay competitive. And so, the winds of change, dear reader, may be blowing in your favor.

This book is organized based on 9 Lenses to help you look before you leap, seven of which are the reasons employees leave, as described above. The first two Lenses--What Do I Want? and How Do I Search for the Right Job and Employer, are vitally important prerequisites for the other seven. We begin with a chapter on knowing yourself—your strengths, weaknesses, interests, enthusiasms, values, preferences, needs and wants--the vitally important first half of the employee-employer equation.

We then move on to the Lens on how to search for and find the right employer, a proven process that is based on systematic research and networking that will result in your identifying enough targeted prospective employers so that your best-fit employer is likely to be among them.

Next, we introduce the Lenses representing the most common reasons employees disengage and leave, with a chapter devoted to each, including key issues, challenges, tips, checklists, warning signs, and questions to ask. You will no doubt discover that one or two of these Lenses are more important than the others to your engagement and job satisfaction.

At the end of each Lens, you will find direct quotations from our interviews with our panel of experts—twenty professionals with years of experience in corporate human resources, employee engagement, recruiting, hiring, executive search, career transition/job search consulting, the future of work, effective communication, diversity & inclusion, corporate ethics, workplace engagement technology/research, and work/family support. You will find our experts' different perspectives, insights, and hard-earned wisdom well worth considering as you contemplate your next step.

Introducing Our Panel of 20 Experts:

Renny Arensberg, VP, Employee Engagement, KVC Healthcare

Ed Baldwin, Founder of HRO Partners, (Human Resource Consulting)

Sherry Benjamins, President, S. Benjamins & Company, Career Coach/Learning Group Facilitator

Dr. Rick Beyer, Founder and CEO, Integritas, LLC, Former Secretary of Labor, State of Kansas (Human Resource Consulting)

Gary Bolles, Author, *The Next Rules of Work* and Chair for the Future of Work at Singularity University

Dennis Boyer, Chairman, Chairman (retired), PrestonClarke & Co. Retained Executive Search

Mark Anthony Dyson, Founder/Host, *The Voice of Job Seekers* Podcast

Bill Ellermeyer, Founder, Ellermeyer Connect (Career Transition Coaching)

Mark Ernst, Managing Principal, Ernst Enterprises (HR Consulting)

Andrea Hendricks, Vice President of Diversity and Inclusion, Cerner Corporation

Bill Holland, Founder/Principal, College-to-Career Catalyst

Cherie Kerr, President of ExecuProv (Communications Training)

Anne Maltese, Director of People Insights, Quantum Workplace (Employee Engagement Software)

Ron Nash, Career Coach

Dr. Lynne Nelleman, Former Member, Glass Ceiling Commission for Presidents Bush and Clinton

Alice Peterson, Founder and Principal, The Loretto Group, and Corporate Ethics Consultant

Steve Puente, CEO, Puente HR (Consulting)

Janet Shouse, The Vanderbilt Kennedy University Center for Excellence in Developmental Disabilities

Gordon Smith, Senior Partner, Mullikin Group (Career Transition Consulting

Mary Kay Ziniewicz, Founder, Bus Stop Mamas (Work-Family Support Systems)

If You Are Still Employed…

How to Know When It's Time to Quit (and The Right Way to Quit)

So, you've had a bad day at work, or perhaps you've had several bad days, or weeks. It's important to know the difference between ordinary, occasional dissatisfaction and the final realization that you are hopelessly mismatched. Our goal here is to help you know when you are truly ready to move on and to advise you how to depart gracefully and in good standing.

How One Employee Knew It Was Time to Quit (Text Exchange Posted on Twitter)

Boss:

"Good evening: I was reviewing the cameras from our shift today and noticed that you were sitting on a stool for most of your shift. This is completely unacceptable behavior, and we will be discussing it tomorrow before shift."

Employee:

"I cleared it with (Lead). I have 2 broken bones in my left foot (doctor documented).

Aside from that - I packed 240+UPH for the entirety of my shift, 12 full hours. I'm not sure if you are aware, but we do have a ranked list for packing displayed directly above our stations. My efforts earned me first place today.

So, just to be clear - my impressive performance was overshadowed by the fact that I wasn't uncomfortable enough while doing it?"

Boss:

"I'm not appreciating your attitude. You could have just said the first part where it was cleared with another lead instead of being disrespectful. This type of behavior isn't going to get you anywhere here."

Employee:

"Hey, thanks for wasting my precious off time with some garbage you didn't bother to investigate beforehand.

Seriously - 240+UPH - what you claim to be the pinnacle of performance there, I achieved it, and I get grief because I was sitting while doing it. You guys need to get your priorities straight. It is no wonder that you have such difficulty retaining staff.

I'm not concerned with going 'anywhere' there. It's a toxic environment with ignorant people at the helm. I won't be in tomorrow or ever again."

Boss:

"We don't need to rush to you leaving. Let's talk in the morning and we can sort this out."

Employee:

"No thanks. Have a good life."

While we don't recommend quitting a job via text and we might suggest using somewhat different language, we certainly appreciate the authenticity of this situation and this employee's frustration. It is a prime example of the "triggering event" (aka "last straw") phenomenon that usually occurs in a sudden (or even gradual) decision to quit.

Signs it may be time to quit

Before getting specific about your current situation, here are some common signals that it **may** be the right time for you to leave…check all that apply (although any one of them may be reason enough):

___You are underutilizing your best strengths and talents.
___You have watched all the good assignments go to others and you believe the boss doesn't trust your judgment or capabilities.
___You are consistently called on to do the grunt work that others don't want to do.
___You no longer feel a sense of mission or purpose in your job.
___You have lost your enthusiasm for the work.
___You don't want your boss's job.
___Your work environment or culture has become toxic or unhealthy.
___You have pursued and exhausted all available opportunities for career growth.
___Your personal and/or family life is suffering because of your job.
___You want to retire and pursue other life interests.
___You are being underpaid compared to others in similar positions or the value you are creating.
___Your skills and expertise are outdated, and you have no interest in further training.
___You can no longer tolerate working for your current boss and there is no acceptable option for getting a new manager.
___Your employer has fallen on hard times and could go out of business.
___You have irresolvable ethical or moral differences with your employer.
___Management is ignoring your ideas, overlooking your efforts, and shutting you out of meetings and important discussions.
___Your peers are making you feel isolated, gossiped about, and excluded.
___Your office, work environment, or resources are substandard compared to your peers'.
___You are so unhappy or stressed that you are losing sleep, getting sick, and dread going to work.
___You have been in your role for a year or more and haven't had a performance discussion or review with your manager.
___Your performance is stagnating despite your best efforts.
___You are up against an impossible task and consistently underperforming.

If more than a few of these signals apply to you and have been obvious for a while, then alarm bells should be going off. Most people stay too long in bad situations because most managers are more prone to keeping us in roles where our performance is acceptable instead of matching us up to our ideal jobs.

Many of us are surprisingly unwilling to move on even if we are miserable. Change is scary, especially when those around us keep telling us we are lucky to have a job. Making a change can seem like too great a risk, but the greater risk may be staying where you are. The right time to get out is before you do serious damage to your health or get so down on yourself that you can't be upbeat in a job interview.

Take time to reflect.

Think about what attracted you to the job and employer when you decided to join up. What was it you were excited about? The career opportunity? The bump in salary? A shorter commute? The friends who were already working there? What has changed to make you begin thinking about quitting? Are one or more of those initial attractions less important to you now?

The exercises and inventories in Lens #1 will allow you to complete a Decision Grid where you can evaluate your current job (and other job options) on Your "Must-Have" Work-Life Needs. Using the Decision Grid, you will assign points to your current job for the needs you prioritized highest. You may discover that you have rated certain needs lower or higher than what you would have rated them when you took the job.

Take a few moments now to reflect, then write your thoughts below about how your criteria for job satisfaction may have changed since you took the job:

____

____

____

____

As a rule, it is advisable to stay in your current job and try to change things for the better, whether that means having a frank conversation with the boss about your performance, how you are perceived, and what you can achieve in your role. You may be able to move laterally into a new position, change your attitude, or adjust your expectations if they are unrealistic.

You will find the Personal Power Grid **in our chapter on Keeping Yourself Engaged to** be useful as you consider your options. Knowing what is and isn't possible for you to control or influence is crucial. What may at first appear to be an unbearable interpersonal conflict with a peer, for example, may instead be your own insecurity about whether you can manage or overcome it without quitting.

What actions could you take?

List below the actions that are now available to you that, if you took them, could change your situation for the better and, if successful, could get you re-engaged and make you want to stay:

1. ____
2. ____
3. ____
4. ____
5. ____

Now list any obstacles you will have to overcome in taking these actions:

1. ____
2. ____
3. ____

Do these obstacles seem worth the effort to overcome them or not? Do they seem insurmountable, or not? Are you ready to invest the energy in overcoming them? Now is probably a good time to have a discussion with a trusted mentor, counselor, or your significant other.

Before you make the final decision to leave, think about the possible downsides. If you have a record of changing jobs more frequently than normal, the risk is that prospective employers may speculate that your serial "job-hopping" indicates an interpersonal issue or they may question whether you will stay long in the job.

The right way to leave

Let's say that you have taken actions to improve things in your current job, allowed a reasonable amount of time for things to get better, that things haven't gotten better, and that you are now ready to move on. Before you quit, here are a few guidelines for making your departure as graceful and professional as possible.

1. Don't discuss your intention to leave with your coworkers.
2. Make sure you have been thorough in your self-assessment process (Lens #1). Do you feel clear about what you want and the kind of work culture you want to join? As many of our expert panelists will testify, it is better to leave when you are going toward a clear and exciting new goal than to get away from a bad situation.
3. Update your resume, create a list of references, organize your list of contacts, and update your LinkedIn and Facebook profiles.
4. Follow the job search process outlined in Lens #2, pursuing all available job search methods, job sites, listings, referral sources, and, if appropriate, part-time, temporary, or consulting opportunities.

5. Conduct your search on your own time, not while in the office or on company time and on your personal/home computer.
6. Be careful not to suddenly change your work habits, such as arriving later, leaving earlier, or dressing noticeably differently for lunchtime job interviews. Stay friendly with peers and remain a team player. Stay as enthusiastic as you can until the day you leave.
7. Once you know what your last day will be, you should give notice to your manager and do everything possible to make things easier for your successor, whoever that may be. Do not burn a bridge. It is not unheard of for employers to hire good people back.

Remember, you have worked hard to create a good reputation at your current employer. You owe it to yourself and to your employer to make your transition to your next job as seamless as possible.

But to avoid getting the cart before the horse, we suggest you proceed straight to Lens #1.

Lens # 1:

Who Am I
and What Do I Really Want?

Your next job is only one half of the best-fit equation. The other half is YOU.

Before reviewing the reasons you might leave an employer, it is important that you first take an honest and thorough look at yourself. Our hope is that you will then have an effective template for evaluating how well future employers might fit YOU instead of trying to "fold, spindle, and mutilate" yourself in a vain attempt to fit into the wrong job or employer.

Leigh Discovers What's Missing

After a stint in the Army, Leigh returned to finish his master's degree in journalism/advertising and went to work as an ad agency copy/contact representative. He loved the creativity of the work that had attracted him to the field in the first place, but after a few months he began to feel that something undefinable was missing. He didn't feel the enthusiasm for the job that he expected to feel, but he didn't know why. He slowly began to realize that the job felt meaningless to him. How was the world any better off, he asked himself, by helping the agency's banking or fast-food clients attract a few more customers away from the competition?

When he began reading Richard N. Bolles' classic career change guide, *What Color is Your Parachute?* it dawned on Leigh what was missing—he had a job, but he needed a calling. The job and career he had chosen was right for some, but not for him. What he didn't know about himself, and had to learn by trial and error, was that he is more fulfilled by work that improves the lives of others in a more personally meaningful way. So, after four years in the ad agency business, and to the astonishment of his friends and relatives, Leigh resigned his job and enrolled in a master's degree program to become a career and job search counselor. He has never regretted that decision.

The Self You Don't Know

The quadrants below* represent various states of self-knowledge. Leigh's need to help others find the right job and career was not known to himself prior to working in advertising, nor was it known to others, so it is an example of the quadrant marked "Unknown". Leigh had another realization in his ad agency job—coworkers would gravitate to his office, open up to him about their problems, and seek out his advice and perspective. Leigh had never thought of himself as a good listener and would not have said out loud that he had good listening skills until his experience winning the trust of his coworkers made him more aware. This is an example of having talents that are so central to our personalities that we fail to value or even see them as talents—they are Blind to us.

When it comes to finding one's place in the work world, the failure to recognize the Blind and Unknown aspects of our personalities can lead to years in the wrong jobs and with the wrong employers.

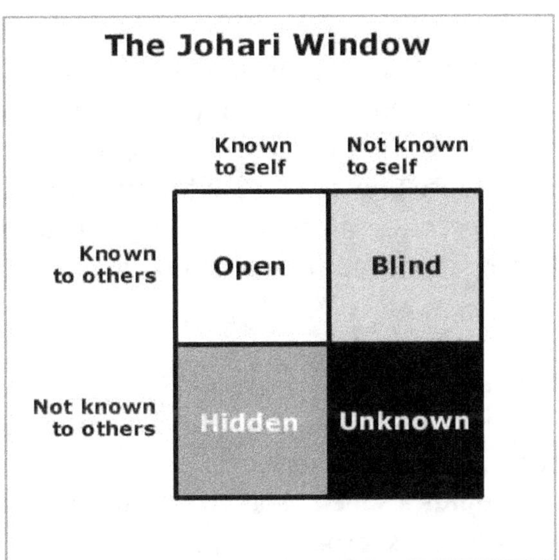

This feedback/disclosure model of self-awareness was developed by psychologists, Joseph Luft and Harry Ingham at the University of California in 1955.

Our hidden talents are also worth acknowledging. Leigh was aware from childhood that he had a talent for drawing. His mother even encouraged him to pursue commercial art and arranged for him to have art lessons when he was fifteen, but he was too interested in baseball at that age to take his artwork seriously. Now he is taking oil painting lessons and has created several canvases he is proud of.

The STRENGTHS and TALENTS YOU KNOW

As we enter the work world or prepare for our next job, it is important to take stock of our strengths and talents. Most likely, you already know what most of your strengths are. Think about what you have always been naturally good at, and what other people have said you are good at.
Grab a pen or pencil now and list below what you consider your greatest strengths or talents:

__________________________________   __________________________________

__________________________________   __________________________________

__________________________________   __________________________________

__________________________________   __________________________________

__________________________________   __________________________________

ALL YOUR STRENGTHS and TALENTS

 After years as career counselors to hundreds of people, we know that the best way to see all our talents clearly is to look back and see how they show up in our most satisfying life accomplishments. We have worked with hundreds of people who were blind to some of their greatest strengths simply because they took them for granted. That is why we strongly recommend you recall, list, describe, and analyze your most satisfying life and career accomplishments to fully appreciate, perhaps for the first time, _all_ your strengths and talents.

Recalling Your Satisfying Achievements:

Cast aside all modesty. Many times in your life you have done things that gave you a deep-down feeling of satisfaction, accomplishment, and pride. Other people may not have taken note of what you did, but it **holds a special and vivid place in your memory**. You may have had lesser and greater accomplishments throughout your life. Some of your accomplishments happened in work settings, while others happened at home, with family or friends, in school settings, during leisure pursuits, while travelling, or in your childhood.

For the following exercise, a **Satisfying Achievement** is anything you:
- …Did well,
- Enjoyed doing,
- Are proud of **(doesn't have to be impressive to others!)**, and
- Can describe as a story--step-by-step, how you did it.

Examples:
- Made my own Halloween costume (age 7)
- Solved the Rubik's Cube (age 12)
- Saved for, researched, negotiated for, and bought a new car (age 17)
- Completed a client project under budget and 30 days earlier than expected (age 28)
- Mediated a conflict between two co-workers (age 34)
- Coached little league team to championship (age 41)

Listing Your Achievements Made Easier:

It is usually easier to remember your satisfying achievements if you divide your life up to now into 10-year segments and into three areas—education, work, and leisure/family.

Using the Life/Work Achievement Recall Grid, list as many accomplishments, big and small, as you can recall in the spaces provided. You will probably recall two or more achievements in some spaces and none in others. Write only two or three words to make note of each achievement. Examples: Negotiated for and bought my first car", "Mediated a conflict between two family members". Give yourself hours or days to come up with as many as you can. Most people can recall and list 10-20 achievements on the grid.

Life/Work Achievement Recollection Grid

Age	Education	Work	Leisure/Family
Birth-10			
11-20			
21-30			
31-40			
41-50			
51-60+			

Describing your Achievements

To truly see and believe in your strengths you must tell stories that provide all the evidence you need. The Achievement Story format that follows provides the necessary space for you to tell your stories. Seven achievement stories are usually enough to recall in enough detail so you can clearly see a pattern of strengths and satisfactions that appear and reappear in your life over the years. You will be richly rewarded with insights by investing time in describing **at least your five most satisfying achievements, (**although seven is recommended for seeing the patterns most clearly.) Make as many copies of the Achievement Story page as you need.

Achievement Story #____

Title____

Your age at the time: ______

Describe the Situation, Opportunity and/or Challenge You Were Facing:

____
____
____

What did you do and…How did you do it, specifically—step-by-step?

Include your initial goal, difficulties you encountered and how you overcame them. What role did you play? What decisions did you make? Was there a turning point? Paint a picture of HOW you did it:

Step 1.____
Step 2.____
Step 3.____
Step 4.____
Step 5.____
Step 6.____
Step 7.____
Step 8.____
Step 9.____
Step 10.____

What was the Outcome...and Why was it Satisfying?

(Describe the feeling you felt at the completion of the achievement, keeping in mind that in some achievements, the outcome is far more satisfying than the process of achieving, and in other achievements, the process is more satisfying):

____
____
____

What strengths, talents, and personality traits did you use/exhibit in this achievement?

____

____

____

We all tend to be modest to the point of being blind at times when it comes to acknowledging our strengths. You may see better words to describe some of your strengths and talents in the inventory below. ***Put a check mark next to the strengths and talents you used in any one of your seven achievements.*** As you go, make note of the strengths and talents you especially enjoyed using by *putting an extra check mark next to those.*

Your Strengths and Talents Inventory

A. LEARNING

______Learn quickly   ______Learn by reading/study
______Grasp concepts   ______Learn by listening
______Learn by example   ______Willingness to seek feedback
______Learn by doing   ______Willingness to seek self-improvement
______Other:

B. RESEARCH/ANALYSIS

______Sense keenly/notice/curiosity   ______Identify the problem/root cause/source
______Research/gather data   ______Analyzing cause and effect
______Compare/distinguish   ______Troubleshoot/test solutions
______Question/interview   ______Persist to find the solution
______Organize data/classify   ______Evaluate/learn from process
______Other:

C. CREATING/INNOVATING

______See connections between ideas   ______Improvise resourcefully
______Synthesize data   ______Visualize/design/create art
______Conceive new ideas   ______Develop new products, processes,
                                                       programs, systems, etc.
______Invent/create   ______Adept with computer graphics
______Other:

D. HUMAN RELATIONS

______Show empathy/sensitivity   ______Show tact/diplomacy
______Be a team player/cooperate   ______Help/serve others
______Display warmth/sociability   ______Counsel/guide others
______Build/inspire trust   ______Interview others well
______Other:

E. SPEAKING

______Listen well
______Express thoughts clearly
______Express feelings assertively
______Give and take feedback freely
______Speak effectively in public
______Other:

______Keep others informed
______Contribute to group discussions
______Communicate in a positive way
______Use language well
______Use humor/entertain/tell stories

F. WRITING

______Write clearly
______Write concisely
______Write persuasively
______Other:

______Proofread/edit
______Take good notes
______Illustrate graphically

G. TEACHING/TRAINING

______Prepare/design training well
______Get participants involved
______Speak with authoritative knowledge
______Explain things clearly
______Other:

______Control time/process
______Convey enthusiasm
______Illustrate concepts vividly
______Maintain interest throughout
______Facilitate group discussion

H. INFLUENCING OTHERS

______Build rapport/trust
______Understand others' self-interest/needs
______Understand others' perspectives
______Sell/persuade
______Other:

______Promote/advertise
______Attract/Recruit talent
______Manage/resolve conflict
______Negotiate effectively
______Customer relations

I. LEADERSHIP

______Take charge/take the initiative
______Build a compelling vision
______Initiate change/take risks
______Gain followers for a vision or goal
______Other:

______Stay focused on results
______Confront tough issues
______Use power appropriately
______Inspire/motivate

J. PLANNING

______Anticipate/analyze problem
______Set realistic goals
______Develop effective strategy/plan
______Other

______Prioritize tasks well
______Set realistic schedule
______Establish measures for success

K. ORGANIZING

______Establish logical systems/processes

______Organize data/information

______Organize people and tasks

______Bring order out of chaos

______Budget and manage finances

______Apply a wide range of computer skills.

______Other:

L. MANAGING PEOPLE

______Communicate expectations

______Recognize/reward

______Delegate tasks

______Confront/manage non-performance

______Oversee and track progress

______Coach/develop others

______Appraise performance/give feedback

______Build teamwork

______Other:

M. WORKING WITH NUMBERS/FINANCES

______Calculate/figure

______Operate computers

______Manage money/budgets

______Conduct audits

______Do accounting/bookkeeping

______Handle purchasing

______Do cost analysis/projections

______Find ways to minimize costs

______Other:

______Analyze/interpret survey data

N. EXECUTING/FOLLOWING THROUGH

______Implement decisions

______Attend to details

______Arrange/coordinate

______Deal with the unexpected

______Expedite

______Get things done/persist

______Check/monitor progress

______Balance details with the big picture

______Other:

O. MANUAL/PHYSICAL

______Eye/hand/foot coordination

______Fix/repair machines

______Hand/finger dexterity

______Build/assemble

______Operate /maintain machines

______Physical strength/agility/stamina

______Refinish/Paint

______Precision working

______Gardening

______Efficient Handling/Expediting

______Other:

______Caring for/Working with Animals

List the talents you most want to use now:

Now look back at the strengths and talents that you double-checked and highlight or circle the ones you most want to use in your future working life.
Then, on the lines below list in order the ones you most want to use in your next job or career endeavor.

1. ____
2. ____
3. ____
4. ____
5. ____
6. ____
7. ____
8. ____
9. ____
10. ____

Now list the talents you most want to improve:

1. ____
2. ____
3. ____
4. ____
5. ____

Congrats on getting this far!

Now, we expand our focus to the broader personality traits that most define you and hold the key to your future success.

Begin by completing the following inventory.

Strengths of Personality and Character—An Inventory

Check all the traits below that describe you. Consider how you may have demonstrated these characteristics in your life and career achievements. Then go back **and circle** the ten (10) that you believe describe you best.

___Accurate	___Imaginative	___Responsible
___Adventurous	___Independent	___Responsive
___Ambitious	___Intuitive	___Results-oriented
___Artistic	___Kind	___Self-assured
___Assertive	___Leader	___Self-aware
___Bold	___Level-headed	___Self-controlled
___Careful	___Logical	___Self-motivated
___Challenging	___Loyal	___Sense of humor
___Civic minded	___Mature	___Sensitive
___Committed	___Methodical	___Shrewd
___Compassionate	___Open-minded	___Sincere
___Confident	___Optimistic	___Sociable
___Conscientious	___Orderly	___Spontaneous
___Cooperative	___Original	___Stable
___Courageous	___Patient	___Steady
___Creative	___Perceptive	___Strong-willed
___Curious	___Perfectionist	___Tactful
___Dedicated	___Personable	___Team-oriented
___Dependable	___Persuasive	___Tenacious
___Determined	___Physically fit	___Thoughtful
___Direct	___Pleasant	___Thrifty
___Disciplined	___Polished	___Tolerant
___Easy-going	___Practical	___Tough-minded
___Efficient	___Precise	___Trustworthy
___Emotional	___Principled	___Unassuming
___Empathetic	___Productive	___Uncomplaining
___Energetic	___Progressive	___Unpretentious
___Entertaining	___Punctual	___Unselfish
___Enthusiastic	___Questioning	___Wise
___Expressive	___Rational	___Witty
___Fair	___Realistic	___Other__________
___Friendly	___Reasonable	___Other__________
___Happy	___Relaxed	___Other__________
___Hard-working	___Reserved	
___Honest	___Resilient	
___Honorable	___Respectful	

We strongly suggest you invite one or more people who know you well to look at the traits you checked **and** circled, then give you the benefit of their perspective.

Another helpful resource is the **Holland Occupational Personality Type** assessment which is available in a Career Interests Game through the University of Missouri's Career Interests Game at https://career.missouri.edu/career-interests-game.

We also draw your attention to **The Myers-Briggs Type Indicator** (MBTI) here because it is the most widely used assessment in the world. Taking it and discovering your type can help support your personal well-being and professional performance by providing you with a deeper understanding of what makes you *you*. With these insights you can make more informed decisions, communicate better with others, and build stronger relationships.

The graph below shows the 16 MBTI personality types. As you scan them, you will probably identify with two or perhaps more. These descriptions are an emphatic testament to the diversity of personalities that make up most workplaces, making it even more obvious why understanding and accepting basic differences is vital for your career success, getting along with coworkers, and for smooth teamwork.

You may take the MBTI online at www.mbtionline/myersbriggsonline and receive an interpretation of your results and additional guidance at their official website. There are many other such assessments—the Big Five, Hogan, the Thomas-Kilmann Conflict Mode inventory, the FIRO-B (personality and team dynamics), DISC Assessment, StrengthsFinder 2.0, The Birkman Method, PrinciplesYou.com, MotivationCode.com, and many others. All are best understood with the assistance of a trained interpreter/counselor.

	Sensing Types		Intuitive Types	
Introverts	**ISTJ** Serious, quiet, earn success by concentration and thoroughness. Practical, orderly, matter-of-fact, logical, realistic, and dependable. See to it that everything is well organized. Take responsibility. Make up their own minds as to what should be accomplished and work toward it steadily, regardless of protests or distractions.	**ISFJ** Quiet, friendly, responsible, and conscientious. Work devotedly to meet their obligations. Lend stability to any project or group. Thorough, painstaking, accurate. Their interests are usually not technical. Can be patient with necessary details. Loyal, considerate, perceptive, concerned with how other people feel.	**INFJ** Succeed by perseverance, originality, and desire to do whatever is needed or wanted. Put their best efforts into their work. Quietly forceful, conscientious, concerned for others. Respected for their firm principles. Likely to be honored and followed for their clear visions as to how best to serve the common good.	**INTJ** Have original minds and great drive for their own ideas and purposes. Have long-range vision and quickly find meaningful patterns in external events. In fields that appeal to them, they have a fine power to organize a job and carry it through. Skeptical, critical, independent, determined, have high standards of competence and performance.
	ISTP Cool onlookers—quiet, reserved, observing and analyzing life with detached curiosity and unexpected flashes of original humor. Usually interested in cause and effect, how and why mechanical things work, and in organizing facts using logical principles. Excel at getting to the core of a practical problem and finding the solution.	**ISFP** Retiring, quietly friendly, sensitive, kind, modest about their abilities. Shun disagreements, do not force their opinions or values on others. Usually do not care to lead but are often loyal followers. Often relaxed about getting things done because they enjoy the present moment and do not want to spoil it by undue haste or exertion.	**INFP** Quiet observers, idealistic, loyal. Important that outer life be congruent with inner values. Curious, quick to see possibilities, often serve as catalysts to implement ideas. Adaptable, flexible, and accepting unless a value is threatened. Want to understand people and ways of fulfilling human potential. Little concern with possessions or surroundings.	**INTP** Quiet and reserved. Especially enjoy theoretical or scientific pursuits. Like solving problems with logic and analysis. Interested mainly in ideas, with little liking for parties or small talk. Tend to have sharply defined interests. Need careers where some strong interest can be used and useful.
Extraverts	**ESTP** Good at on-the-spot problem solving. Like action, enjoy whatever comes along. Tend to like mechanical things and sports, with friends on the side. Adaptable, tolerant, pragmatic; focused on getting results. Dislike long explanations. Are best with real things that can be worked, handled, taken apart, or put together.	**ESFP** Outgoing, accepting, friendly, enjoy everything and make things more fun for others by their enjoyment. Like action and making things happen. Know what's going on and join in eagerly. Find remembering facts easier than mastering theories. Are best in situations that need sound common sense and practical ability with people.	**ENFP** Warmly enthusiastic, high-spirited, ingenious, imaginative. Able to do almost anything that interests them. Quick with a solution for any difficulty and ready to help anyone with a problem. Often rely on their ability to improvise instead of preparing in advance. Can usually find compelling reasons for whatever they want.	**ENTP** Quick, ingenious, good at many things. Stimulating company, alert and outspoken. May argue for fun on either side of a question. Resourceful in solving new and challenging problems, but may neglect routine assignments. Apt to turn to one new interest after another. Skillful in finding logical reasons for what they want.
	ESTJ Practical, realistic, matter-of-fact, with a natural head for business or mechanics. Not interested in abstract theories; want learning to have direct and immediate application. Like to organize and run activities. Often make good administrators; are decisive, quickly move to implement decisions; take care of routine details.	**ESFJ** Warm-hearted, talkative, popular, conscientious, born cooperators, active committee members. Need harmony and may be good at creating it. Always doing something nice for someone. Work best with encouragement and praise. Main interest is in things that directly and visibly affect people's lives.	**ENFJ** Responsive and responsible. Feel real concern for what others think or want, and try to handle things with due regard for the other's feelings. Can present a proposal or lead a group discussion with ease and tact. Sociable, popular, sympathetic. Responsive to praise and criticism. Like to facilitate others and enable people to achieve their potential.	**ENTJ** Frank, decisive, leaders in activities. Develop and implement comprehensive systems to solve organizational problems. Good in anything that requires reasoning and intelligent talk, such as public speaking. Are usually well informed and enjoy adding to their fund of knowledge.

Your Potential Derailers

We strongly advocate keeping focused on your strengths and talents as you seek a new job or other career move. Yet, we all need to acknowledge the personal tendencies (aka weaknesses) that may have been career-limiting for us in the past and could derail us again. This is where it is all-important to be honest with yourself. Recognizing, acknowledging, and learning to manage our potential derailers can become an actual strength as we go forward. Most people can easily identify a handful of weaknesses among the list below that may have been career limiting in the past.

Place a check next to the common derailers below that could be a problem for you going forward:

______Avoiding conflict at all costs
______Bullying
______Blaming others, victim mentality
______Dishonesty
______Your way or the highway
______Raising your voice, excessive anger
______Low self-confidence, self-doubt
______Failure to express appreciation
______Making excuses
______Not listening
______Pushing yourself and others too hard
______Needing to win at all costs
______Claiming credit you don't deserve
______Unwillingness to compromise
______Taking a negative or oppositional view
______Gossiping, hoarding information to gain power
______Overconfidence, taking ill-advised risks
______Failure to take advisable risks
______Failure to keep confidences
______Being a know-it-all, showing how smart you are
______Sarcasm/deriding/disrespecting others
______Sacrificing integrity for personal gain
______Overwhelming others with your intensity
______Failure to pay attention to office politics
______Lack of assertiveness, failure to speak up
______Impatience, expecting immediate gratification
______Deciding with your head, not your heart
______Overly rational, lacking in empathy
______Giving unwanted opinions or advice
______Judging others, imposing your standards
______Expecting perfection
______Succumbing to flattery, playing favorites

______Failure to apologize
______Anxiety-driven fear of making mistakes/decisions

Now circle or highlight 3-5 derailers that you feel you most need to guard against in your near future.

We strongly recommend you discuss your potential derailers with someone who knows you well to get the benefit of their perspective.

Past Job Likes and Dislikes

One of the most popular and insightful ways to interview a job candidate is to ask the person to describe what he or she liked most about all previous jobs. This review is not only insightful for those who may interview you, it can be even more insightful for you.

In the spaces below list your previous jobs (paid or unpaid, regardless of your age) and what you liked most and least about each one.

First Job: **Liked Most**   **Liked Least**

____

Next Job:

____

Next Job:

____

Next Job:

____

Next Job:

____

Next Job:

____

Next Job:

Next Job:

Next Job:

Next Job:

Next Job:

Next Job:

Next Job:

Next Job:

Do You Notice Any Patterns?

Describe below what pattern(s) you see in the types of situations and challenges where you are inspired to be your best as well as the kinds of working conditions that are less comfortable or undesirable and don't bring out the best in you. What management styles, for example, do you respond to positively and negatively?

____
____
____
____
____

List Any "Dream Jobs" You Have Thought Of:

____
____
____
____
____

Another revealing question we career counselors ask our clients is:
"What do you like to do when no one is telling you what to do?"

List 20 things you like to do outside of work:

1. ____
2. ____
3. ____
4. ____
5. ____
6. ____
7. ____
8. ____
9. ____
10. ____
11. ____
12. ____
13. ____
14. ____
15. ____
16. ____
17. ____
18. ____
19. ____
20. ____

What patterns do you see? Are you mostly alone or with people? What challenges do you respond to? What interests reappear? What strengths and talents are involved that you would like to use more or improve? What areas of knowledge do you want to deepen? Do you see talents, interests, enthusiasms, and activities you would like to pursue more extensively in your working life?

Describe whatever insights you have gained from this exercise:

____
____
____
____
____

Your Areas of Knowledge/Expertise:

List the areas where you have acquired knowledge via formal or informal learning:

____
____
____
____

Now go back and circle or highlight the knowledge areas above you most want to use in your next job.

Finally, list any new or long-standing areas of interest that you are enthusiastic about and would like to research more:

____
____
____

Your Work-Life Preferences

Now, with the benefit of hindsight, you are ready to begin profiling the attributes of the employer or employers that will be your best-fit target for your next move.
Place a check next to the descriptors in each category below that are important to you now:

The Organization

___Industry leader	___Fast-growing	___Allows flextime
___Pays for performance	___Ethical	___Strong healthcare benefits
___Family-oriented	___Promotes from within	___Secure/stable future
___Has childcare	___Privately held	___Nationwide audiences
___Small employer (>50)	___Medium (50-500)	___Large employer (500+)
___Consumer/retail	___Wholesale business	___Desirable location
___Competitive/fair pay	___Caring culture	___Results culture
___Allows work from home	___Other______________	___Other______________

The Physical Environment

___New/modern	___Free/adequate parking	___Safe/secure surroundings
___Private office	___Quiet work area	___On-site gym or access
___Company car	___Up-to-date technology	___No relocation required
___Reasonable commute	___Smoke-free	___Safe
___Work from home	___Other______________	___Other______________

Your Manager

___Clear goals/objectives	___Gives honest feedback	___Open to change
___Decisive leadership	___Visionary	___Participative
___Good delegator	___Accessible	___Competent/knowledgeable
___Team builder	___Frank/candid	___Handles conflict well
___Fair	___Respectful	___Gives praise/recognition
___Values learning	___Coaches effectively	___Encourages innovation
___Values diversity	___Other______________	___Other______________

The Working Conditions

___Fast-paced	___Set my own hours/pace	___Regular/set hours
___Overtime available	___Work independently	___Close collaboration
___Informal dress	___Business dress	___Support services available
___Frequent travel	___Limited travel	___Limited administrivia
___Work with the public	___Other____________	___Other____________

The Work Itself

___Uses my best strengths	___Meaningful work	___High risk/high reward
___Work mainly with people	___Work mainly with data	___Work mainly with physical things
___See immediate results	___Definite outcomes	___High task variety and change
___Move around	___Highly structured	___Precision required
___Work under pressure	___Other____________	___Other____________

Rewards for Your Efforts

___Help/serve others	___Improve/make better	___Be in charge
___Self-expression	___Master a process/craft	___Gain Status/prestige
___See measurable results	___Learn/gain expertise	___Pioneer/explore
___Overcome odds	___Make big decisions	___Solve challenging problems
___Acquire wealth	___Mentor others	___Contribute to society
___Have job security	___Advance/Be promoted	___Have power/influence
___Compete and win	___Create beauty/art	___Start something new
___Intellectual stimulation	___Gain recognition	___Other____________

Lifestyle

___Live an exciting life	___Live a tranquil life	___Involved in community
___Afford nice things	___Regular vacations	___Be a good parent
___Have work-life balance	___Be financially secure	___Live where I want
___Education for family	___Travel abroad	___Comfortable retirement

___Strong friendships   ___Enjoy good health   ___Loving/caring relationship

___Live amidst beauty   ___Have leisure time   ___Help the less fortunate

___Other_____________   ___Other_____________   ___Other_______________

Now, go back and circle or highlight just your most important preferences in each category.

Your Longer-Range Life-Career Goals:

____
____
____
____
____

Bringing it All into Focus: Your 20 "Must-Haves"

Based on your review of all the previous self-assessments of your talents, personality traits, knowledges, values, longer-term goals, and preferences, list below (in order of importance) the things you most need and want in your ideal job and workplace, keeping in mind that #1 should be the thing you are least willing to trade off:

1. ____
2. ____
3. ____
4. ____
5. ____
6. ____
7. ____
8. ____
9. ____
10. ____
11. ____
12. ____
13. ____
14. ____
15. ____
16. ____
17. ____
18. ____
19. ____
20. ____

Jobs to Pursue

Based on Your 20 "Must-Haves" and considering your longer-range life goals…
List Jobs or Work Roles for Which You Feel Qualified *and Want* to Pursue:

____
____
____
____
____
____
____
____
____

- For further ideas about jobs that might be of interest, we strongly recommend you visit the **O*Net Online** (www.onetonline.org/find or www.onetonline.org/search) , maintained by the U.S. Department of Labor. You will find occupations listed and classified by field, industry, and current/future openings anticipated. You will also find information on skills, abilities and knowledge required, plus insights into best job fit based on your interests, values and other preferences. By using the Content Model (www.onetcenter.org/content.html), you can find several pages of detail on each occupation of interest.

- **Glassdoor.com** releases an annual list of **50 Best Jobs in America** based on three factors that are top of mind for people applying to new jobs: the median salary, the number of open roles across the U.S., and overall job satisfaction. While it is always good to know which jobs have the most openings, pay well, and many others find satisfying, those jobs may not be right for you if they don't satisfy the criteria (talents, values, interests, and preferences) you have identified in the previous exercises.

Now List Your Possible Best-Fit Workplaces:

Drawing on your current level of awareness and knowledge of industries, markets and employers, begin your list of Target Employers--prospective companies/organizations in your geographic target areas.

If you are not sure where to start, Google "best places to work" in your current or desired city. You may also want to check out the following listings:

- Glassdoor.com's annual listing of 100 Best Places to Work
- *Fortune.com* magazine's 100 Great Places to Work

- Quantumworkplace.com's annual Best Places to Work: https://www.quantumworkplace.com/best-companies-to-work-for
- Bestplacestowork.org's Best Places to Work in the Federal Government
- Bizjournal.com for Best Places to Work in a city near you
- Employee reviews of workplaces available on: FairyGodBoss (https://fairygodboss.com/company-reviews); Indeed (https://indeed.com/companies?from=gnav-acme--acme-webapp); Vault (https://www.vault.com/company-ratings-research); and Career Bliss (www.careerbliss.com/reviews).

If you are already employed and are still open to staying where you are for now, list your current employer at the top. As you do your research and gain advice and information from your friends, associates, and those they refer you to, you will add to this list and to your list of possible jobs.

My Target Workplaces

Lens #2:

How Do I Search for the Right Job and Workplace?

This book is all about getting you into the *right* job--with the employer whose culture *fits you*. **The chances of that happening are greatly increased by increasing the number of job opportunities you have available to choose from**. And the chances of having those opportunities are greatly increased when you are using the smartest, most proven job search methods.

There are many excellent books on resume-writing, job interviewing, and salary negotiating and we are happy to recommend some of the best on our website. Our purpose in this chapter is to make sure you are launching your job search down a path that will bring to you the most and the best opportunities from which to choose.

Who's Doing the Hiring?

As you build your target list of prospective workplaces, keep in mind that approximately 85 percent of employers have fewer than 100 employees (see below) and that these smaller employers account for almost two-thirds of all jobs in the U.S. and create more new jobs as well:

Total Employees	Number of Businesses
1 - 4 employees	12,493,536
5 - 9 employees	1,829,875
10 - 19 employees	779,922
20 - 49 employees	467,634
50 - 99 employees	170,749
100 - 249 employees	94,352
250 - 499 employees	33,695
500 - 999 employees	19,000
1,000+ employees	23,553
Uncoded records	1,765,009
Grand Total	17,677,325

Source: NAICS Association, LLC, 2020

Most job seekers are unaware of these facts and often make the mistake of limiting their search to only the employers they have heard of, which usually happen to be the largest. Because so many job seekers make this mistake, you will be facing much stiffer competition if you limit your search to larger, more well-known employers.

Tapping the Hidden Job Market

So, why create a target list at all? Why not just go where the openings are and apply for jobs posted online?

As job search coaches we have heard this question too many times to count. Some job seekers resist creating a target list because it feels like they are limiting their search when in fact they are using the list partly to expand and refine it. Others resist because they are simply impatient, or they have never given much thought to how employers go about filling and creating jobs.

It turns out that employers fill (and often create) about 75 percent of all jobs through the hidden job market—by hiring through trusted personal referrals, and not by posting, listing, or advertising them online or anywhere else. Why? For the same reason that most people would never look for a dentist on Google; instead, they would ask friends and relatives for a referral.

Employers know that when a coworker or some other acquaintance refers a friend or associate to them, that coworker is risking their reputation. If the person they refer does not perform up to snuff, the person doing the hiring will lose trust in them. Hiring the wrong person reflects badly on the hiring manager, so every hire is a risk to their reputation for good judgment. By trusting those who risk their reputations by making the referral, employers reduce the risk of making a bad hire.

By creating a target list of potential employers, you are creating an important tool that you will circulate among your contacts. When you show it to them, it will remind them that they know people at some of your targeted employers. They may even know something about unmet needs within these employers and jobs that may be on the cusp of being created or filled informally. They will also ask why you do not have other employers on your list that they may happen to know are growing and hiring.

Thus, as you become visible to your contacts, your list will grow. You may also learn from your contacts that some companies on your list have undesirable cultures or other problems that will give you reason to consider removing them. Eventually, you will home in on a handful that show the most promise as best-fit destinations for you.

How to Expand and Research Your Target List of Employers

Your list should include employers:
- You have dreamed of working for
- You find on Google or Wikipedia by entering "employers in ___________ industry"
- Where your Linked-In and fellow college alumni contacts work
- Currently listing jobs online (Indeed.com, ZipRecruiter.com, Monster.com, CareerBuilder.com, etc.) and for temporary jobs Google "temp jobs" and the name of your city
- You read about in the news, magazines, and periodicals
- You learn about through your friends and other associates

Your mission is to find out as much as possible about these organizations, so you are that much more informed as you begin and continue your networking campaign. Keep in mind that the highest percentage of job seekers who quit their jobs leave during the first 30 days. Why? Because they didn't do enough research to know how much they would dislike the job or the new employer. As you research and network with your contacts, you will gather enough information to give you reasons to begin prioritizing your list of target employers based on culture, leadership, growth, and your personal preferences and fit factors.

As you visit their websites, you will find that many of them have current open job postings and that some are possible best-fit opportunities for you.

When you discover such postings, it is a good idea to jump-start the networking process by finding someone in your contact database (see next section) who works at the posting employer or may know someone there and be willing to introduce you to the person with the power to hire. They may also be able to provide valuable inside information about the employer's culture, strategic direction, challenges, and talent needs.

Interviewing for "Fresh A-I-R" (Advice, Information, and Referrals)

Interviewing for advice and information within your network of contacts and those to whom they refer you is likely to uncover jobs and possibly better-fit employers that you have not considered.

Follow these steps:

1. List and organize your personal contacts.

A referral to your best-fit employer can come from someone you already know or, from someone *they* know. If you list 100 of your contacts and each of them also knows at least 100 people, you have 10,000 potential contacts. The more people who know about you, the more likely it is that one of them knows of an opportunity that is right for you.

As you begin your list, consider:

- Current coworkers
- Former coworkers
- Neighbors and community relationships
- Customers/Clients
- Friends (old and new), including those you only know from Facebook, Twitter, Instagram, and other social media
- Family
- Vendors, service workers
- Fellow members of associations and clubs
- School and university acquaintances
- Service professionals (doctors, dentists, lawyers, accountants)
- Social organizations
- Other job seekers

Now is a good time to go through any business cards you have collected, the contact database on your cell phone, notes you may have entered on your daily calendar, and anywhere else you have captured a name. You will need to organize your contacts into a filing system using spreadsheet software like Microsoft Excel or Trello that allows you to make notes recording your interactions with them.

As you make your list, try not to judge who will or will not be able to help you. You *will* be surprised. It is natural to reach out to your closest friends and associates because you feel more comfortable talking to them than to those you know less well. Just remember that job referrals most often come from the strangers our friends will introduce to us. We suggest you categorize your growing contact database into three categories:

A's—Friends, relatives, former coworkers, and those you know
well.

B's—Strangers your A contacts will refer you to, some of whom may even have the power to
hire you or refer you to the person who does. As you network with your A contacts, your list of
B contacts will grow rapidly.

C's—Strangers at your developing list of target employers that you identify through your own
systematic online research and who can advocate for you with the person who can hire you.

2. Prepare Your Self-Introduction

The main thing to remember is that even though you are looking for a job, you do not want to
give your contacts the impression that you expect them to have a job for you or know of one. If
they do, great, but don't let them think you expect it. Our contacts usually want to help, but
you must ask them for the kind of help that most are able to give you—Advice, Information,
and Referrals (A-I-R). If you convey in any way that you expect them to have or know of a job,
most will feel bad because they could not help you and the meeting or phone call will soon be
over.

It is usually a good idea to prepare a script for your first few calls, especially those you have not
met...something like this:

*'Hi, Mary, it's Jim Smith. Tom Johnson suggested I contact you. Tom and I worked together at
ABC Company for several years. I just left ABC company and Tom thought you might be a great
source of advice and information as I begin my search for a new job. Please understand I don't
expect you to know of a job, but I would love to get your perspective on the job market, industry
trends, and any ideas, insights, or advice you might have for next steps. If you are open to a
brief phone meeting, I'd like to set up a 15-minute discussion at a time that's convenient for
you."*

If your contact says, "I can talk now," tell them that you would like to send them a list of your
potential target employers (above) first so they can have it in front of them as you discuss the
reasons you have listed them. As they are looking at it, they may recognize employers they
know about and think of contacts who work there. They may also recognize their own
employer's name on the list. If your contact asks for your resume, we suggest you politely
decline. Asking for you to send a resume is often a way for some contacts to get out of having
any further discussion and, by agreeing to send it, you give the impression you were not really
interested in their advice and information after all.

After you have interviewed them for A-I-R and told them more about your background and
talents, they may indeed say they know of a job opportunity, and it may be appropriate at that
point to send your resume. If they say that there is a specific job open in their organization that
sounds like a possible fit for you, pursue the next step of finding out more.

Just keep in mind that following through on the A-I-R interview communicates that you are sincere and selective about finding your best-fit option. Also remember that resumes are generally better left behind after a meeting than sent ahead in hopes of getting an interview. We suggest you never send a resume unless it has been requested.

3. Obtain and Conduct A-I-R Interviews with Your "A" and "B" Contacts

Once you have emailed your target list of employers to your contact, you are ready to conduct an A-I-R phone interview. If you are conducting the interview in person, you can bring the list with you instead of emailing it in advance. It is usually best to Google the contact's employer and visit their website before making the initial call to request the interview. Also remember that it is better not to ask top-level leaders questions that subordinates could have easily answered.

A successful A-I-R interview usually lasts no more than 30 minutes and goes like this:

1. Thank them again for their time.

2. Build rapport briefly with small talk, often related to the person who referred you or whatever else you may have in common. A good question to begin with is "How is your day going so far?"

3. Repeat that you are interested in advice, information, and possible referrals to others who may have information and advice, *but you do not expect them to have or know of a job.*

4. Introduce yourself with a two-minute summary of your work history with emphasis on how you grew and progressed professionally in each job, what you liked most, strengths/talents, you enjoy using, an achievement or two you are proud of, key workplace preferences, why you are interested in your target industries/companies, and your ideal job or job options as you see them. This will be challenging, so prepare by writing your two-minute summary and practice saying it.

5. Start asking your questions, selecting from these for the allotted time:

- How did you get into this field?
- What do you like most about your job and your employer?
- What do you see as the most significant trends you see in this field?
- How do you see the job market right now?
- How do you think my background and talent would fit with employers in this field?
- What advice do you have for me in my job search?
- Do you know of anyone else that you think I should talk to?
- Do you feel comfortable referring me to them?

- Ask them to look at your target list of prospective employers as you describe why you selected the ones you have listed. *Make clear that you are not expecting them to know of an available job at these organizations.* Ask if they happen to be familiar with your listed employers and what they know about them.
- Ask if they know anyone at any of the employers on your target list that might be helpful in your search and whether they feel comfortable referring you to them.
- Ask also if they know of an employer not on the list that you should add to the list.
- Are there any other next steps that you would recommend I take?

6. Thank them for their time and ask if they would mind if you checked in with them in a couple of weeks to let them know about your progress, based on acting on their advice and contacting the referrals they gave you.

7. Always send an email thank you note as soon as you get home.

8. Follow up with an email in two weeks to let them know how you have incorporated their advice into your search and update them on your progress, including your discussions with the individuals to whom they referred you.

9. Set a recurring monthly reminder to send an email to keep each of your contacts updated on your progress.

10. Identify "C" Contacts at Your Target Employers and Email Requests for A-I-R Interviews.

The most direct route to your new job may be to identify contacts at your target employers through your own online research who will agree to an A-I-R discussion and possibly advocate for you with the person who has the power to hire you.

To get started, update your LinkedIn Profile, and follow a process we strongly advocate as detailed in Steve Dalton's excellent book—*The 2-Hour Job Search*:

By browsing LinkedIn Groups and using the "custom search" function, search for LinkedIn members who work at your top ten target employers, preferably people high enough in the organization and with enough experience there to have influence.

On the company pages you can even find information about new hires, job-title changes, job postings, job histories, and even where former employees were re-employed. You can also go to the profile page of schools or colleges you attended and find others who attended there.

LinkedIn requires you to have a paid membership to connect with someone who is not a direct connection.

Try to identify at least two promising contacts at each of your ten targets. These individuals may also be found among your "A" and "B" contacts.

Uncover e-mail addresses for these contacts using an email finder website or service such as Clearbit, Lusha, RocketReach, and LinkedIn's "invitations to connect," then send introductory emails (as you did with "A's" and "B's") to these "C" contacts requesting an A-I-R interview.

We also suggest you set up a Google Alert on your top ten target workplaces, so you can receive regular updates about them.

"If You Work the Process, the Process Will Work"

These are words we have spoken to skeptical job seekers for years before they finally proved it to themselves. The networking process we describe above may seem indirect and time-consuming, but we assure you that if you follow it faithfully, it is the fastest way to find your best-fit opportunity. Because 70 percent of all jobs are found through informal networking, you should spend at least 70% of your time working the networking process.

Don't Take this Journey Alone

Involve your spouse or partner and family in this process, as they have a vested interest.

We know of a situation where the father was discussing his search at dinner with his family. The teenage son commented that he hoped the father would find something in Colorado since they all liked to ski. The teen then went to his computer, searched, and found a prospective employer with an opening that matched his father's experience and objective.
Bottom line--Dad acted and got a very good position in Colorado.

Traditional Methods Can Also Work

As Richard N. Bolles pointed out in his classic job search bestseller, *What Color is Your Parachute?,* job seekers should not overlook traditional methods such as:

- Checking employers' job postings on the internet
- Approaching private employment agencies or contingency search firms
- Answering ads in professional or trade journals in your field
- Joining job-search support groups in your community
- Checking for openings with your state or federal employment office
- Volunteering at a local non-profit
- Doing freelance or contract work
- Asking friends, neighbors, and family if they know of job leads
- Walking in the employer's front door at just the right time

Our cautionary recommendation is that you spend no more than 30 percent of your time on these traditional methods and the rest of your campaign on the systematic process we have outlined above.

Other Job Search Resources

Trello (https://trello.com): An excellent resource is the free project management software, which can help you systematically organize your job search as the serious project it should be.

Indeed.com: Job board with thousands of openings in the U.S.

Proven.com: Lists the best job boards for job seekers at https://blog.proven.com/100-best-job-boards-to-find-niche-talent.

Niche job boards that list vacancies in specific fields and industries (visit www.good.co/blog/list-of-100-niche-job-boards)

Company job boards on their websites under "careers" or "opportunities."

As we mentioned before, this is not primarily a job search book, so we are not including guidance here on resume-writing, responding to job ads and listings, working with employment agencies and search firms, answering common interview questions, and negotiating compensation.

There are many good comprehensive job search books available. Having had decades of experience coaching job seekers into the right jobs, we do have extensive job search resources and we are happy to share those on our website-www.RightJobBetterWorkplace.com. The best way to find a job is to use multiple job search methods, not just the networking process we have outlined above. Answering online postings may also get you a job, although the odds are much lower.

As we have stressed, this is a book about finding the *right* job with the *right* employer. We intend to help you do that by addressing, one at a time, the main reasons employees tend to quit their jobs over the next seven chapters. You will find that one or two of the chapters will be more important and meaningful to you than the others. You may also be surprised to realize that others are more (or less) important to you than you would have first thought. We hope that you will find value in the questions, insights, and tools we provide. Even if you think you know exactly what you want to do and the employer for whom you want to do it...we suggest you always have a Plan B (and C, and D, and so on). Building and expanding your target list will help you create those options and opportunities.

A Cautionary Tale: Joe Buys Himself a Job and a Big Headache

Joe always had a strong work ethic, a strong mechanical aptitude, and had served as a mechanic in the Army. So, when a friend asked him to invest in buying a reputable business that reconditioned used cars for a local dealership, he took the opportunity to be an entrepreneur and become financially independent. He was able and willing to invest financially, and he knew it could take months or years to break even, but after three years of long hours, six days a week, a 45-minute commute in traffic, and the headaches of supervising and rearranging schedules of undependable workers, he started getting terrible migraines.

Then, when the head mechanic had a disabling and grisly accident in the shop, Joe took it as a sign to get out. He and his friend decided to sell the business and were able to break even financially. "I didn't have enough savings in reserve to stick it out," Joe admitted. I should have done more of a due diligence analysis and more detailed questioning of the previous owners before buying into the business. Talking to a few owners of other auto-related businesses might have even warned me away from buying into it in the first place."

What about bias?

Yes, there is bias in the hiring process. Let's discuss.

Each of us offers unique talents, skills, and goals to a potential job. Having said that, employers may not look at each of us through the same lens in terms of those talents and experiences.

Sadly, many of us will experience bias in the hiring process (and once we're on the job, for that matter), and we need to understand the impact of bias in terms of bias getting in the way of achieving our career search goals. As Andrea Hendricks, a successful executive who, as a woman of color, has experienced bias says: "One day I hope we can forget about these differences. In the meantime, it is a difficult challenge to navigate."

It's likely that many reading this book have experienced bias in the workplace, but some groups more commonly experience bias. To name a few kinds of bias:

·Gender. ·Age. ·Ethnicity. ·Disability. ·Sexuality.	·Hair Style. ·Obesity. ·Employment Status. ·Residence. ·Method of Transportation	·Religion. ·Pregnancy. ·Ethnic Fashions. ·Names. ·Affinity Bias.

How we experience bias, in some cases, can change over time. Perhaps you just recently suffered an injury that has left you disabled. Or perhaps you have gotten older and now experience bias because of your age that you didn't experience years before. But the research is clear that some of us will face additional challenges because of bias.

So, what should we do?

Dr. Hendricks rightly advises that "If someone has experienced bias in the past, they have more homework to do to ensure the environment is safe and productive, not only through words but through their actions." We believe that a careful review of each prospective employee using the lenses in the following chapters can improve the chances of securing a job in a culture that works well for everyone."

For more about dealing with and overcoming bias in the workplace, see Appendix A.

Our Expert Panelists Have Advice for Those Seeking a Better Workplace:

Dennis Boyer: *"The pandemic required employers to jettison workers. There is an abundance of top talent on the sidelines now. But some hiring authorities may view things with a more skeptical eye. They likely will scrutinize your reason(s) for leaving or why your job was targeted for layoff. It's an unfair characterization but some employers may look at sidelined people as possible 'C' players. You may experience this prejudice even if it is not overtly expressed. Be prepared to carefully articulate why <u>your position</u> became a casualty. That's an important distinction because in many cases it is the position that was targeted for elimination, not the person. If appropriate, consider asking your former employer if they are willing to prepare a 'Reason-for-Leaving' statement' that explains what happened."*

"There's another aspect of a job search in a post-pandemic time and in an era where job search and executive search has been so relegated to the internet. It can be soulless and depressing work for the jobseeker to be sitting in front of a computer screen, applying for positions, never receiving an acknowledgement, etc. You obviously cannot ignore job postings on the internet, but I would encourage anyone to limit their screen time (maybe 30% to 40% total) and focus the 60% to 70% of their time on personal contact by phone or in person. Make sure that everyone in your personal network has a copy of your resume and knows what you're trying to accomplish. Expand that network. Attend conferences or seminars. Meet new people. Spread favors. <u>Do not</u> sit in front of a computer screen all day long!"

Mark Dyson: *"Based on my interviews and coaching sessions with hundreds of job seekers and job search experts, I offer the following advice:*

- *Don't make the mistake of completely relying on job boards. It's too competitive, and you're not likely to get a response. Network, network, network! Getting referrals may take longer, but they are more likely to get you into a better-fit job.*
- *Master the use of LinkedIn as a research tool to learn about target companies. Learn how to use the company pages where you'll see the employees, their positions, and how you're connected to them. It's possible a network connection is already linked to someone in the company and potentially can introduce you. Note (but not copy) how others present themselves, what titles and relevant expertise language they use to describe themselves.*
- *As you approach companies, seek to uncover the problem your skills can help solve--look below the surface to job title and duties. Be sure you use modern titles and not obsolete ones.*

- *Look for high-profile people in your target companies on YouTube or podcasts. You might be able to quote the CEO during an interview. You might even have the audacity to contact them. More often than not they will pass on your name to be contacted. Who is going to tell the CEO no?*
- *Be prepared to ask a handful of questions during job interviews, but don't ask them all at once. Weave them throughout the conversation. You want to ask them as part of the natural back-and-forth flow.*
- *Realize you will most likely need to have several job opportunities in the queue that are in different stages of development. Since companies conduct as many as 14 interviews during the process, you should continue to interview with 4-6 companies. You'll increase your opportunities to find work quicker than depending on one company to hire you.*
- *Know the trends impacting your target industry and the companies in it.*
- *If you don't have the training required for your targeted job, get it. Make it a cornerstone conversation while networking with those in your industry.*
- *Be selective--look for an employer that cares about you. The pandemic has revealed those who do and those who don't.*
- *Students coming out of school need to identify what they don't know and address their gaps. If you're still in college, take the opportunity to have an extra internship.*
- *If you are facing bias as an older worker looking for a full-time job, try looking for short-term contracting projects to prove yourself.*
- *Dig your well before you need water. In other words, keep your network warm before you have to go looking for your next job."*

Bill Ellermeyer: *"The pandemic drove home to me and my clients the importance of developing and refining their presentation skills on Zoom. We're all broadcasters now, as Cherie Kerr reminds her clients and audiences. We need to record ourselves on video and notice our non-verbal tics, be aware of lighting, the background, the cadence, volume, and tone of our speech, and the confidence we project. I strongly recommend that my job-seeking clients sharpen those skills before starting their screening interviews."*

Mark Ernst: *"Don't run from a job; run toward one. Trust your instincts. If the job or the employer doesn't feel right, don't take the first offer that comes along. If you think you can change them, you probably won't. If you do find yourself in the wrong situation, don't stay too long--no more than three to six months after you know you've made a mistake. If you do stay too long, you risk becoming more bitter and resentful and your values can get out of alignment."*

Bill Holland: *"If you get laid off, use the opportunity to work on things you know you need to deal with and improve so you can tell interviewers what you are doing to make yourself more valuable. Keeping up with new technologies is especially important. Do not shy away from having been laid off. Most employers will understand and will not hold it against you. Do, however, emphasize how you used this time to improve your skills--especially those the employer values."*

Cherie Kerr: *"One of the biggest mistakes people make in job interviews is launching into a canned self-introduction, usually in response to the frequently asked first question 'Tell me about yourself' Keep it short and let the interviewer take the lead. Don't over-prepare and force your points into the conversation. Listen carefully and ask questions on the back end of your answers to keep it a two-way conversation."*

"The greatest enemies of good communication, whether in improv or in interviews, are fear and inhibition. They keep you from thinking fast on your feet. Take the pressure off yourself by realizing that things will be OK even if you don't get the job. Your health, family, and spirituality are more important."

Lynne Nelleman: *"On-campus or Zoom recruiters are often HR professionals, executives coming back to schools from which **they** graduated or mid-level government or military officers seeking very specialized skills or filling quotas. A few slots on sign-up sheets get filled even before they go online. Why? Because calls have been made to deans and professors asking, "who should we see on your campus?" Ask administrative assistants for a 10-minute appointment with your dean. Professors? Introduce yourself before or after classes or in receptions after their announced speeches. Search online for their TED talks, interviews, books, or syllabi. KNOW them."*

"Seek their opinions on industries or companies of interest to you. Start in your sophomore or junior year. Once you begin working on your resume in your senior year, get a copy to them. Ask for feedback. Incorporate suggestions given to you. Follow up with revisions or final content. Add one- or two-line thank you notes. When those 'who should we see on your campus?' calls come in, it's more likely your resume will be the one that goes out! The first step in getting a job is by running on an inside track."

"Once, when I wrote a letter asking for an interview with a company back in my hometown, I was offered a job. Then, suddenly, the company I was with asked me to lead a special six-month project. The project would give me skills well beyond what I had at that moment, so I called to ask for a delayed start date. The response? "We wanted you yesterday, we want you tomorrow, and we will want you six months from now." Talk about my commitment to that employer once I took the job!"

"If there's a receptionist /staff member in the company who helped you, don't hesitate to thank them before you leave or with a follow-up note. "

Steve Puente: *"Many employers have had to cut back on salaries and bonus plans, so you may need to reduce your expectations. Be flexible and persistent. Be willing to go back to working onsite instead of working from home. Don't give up. Work steadily on your job search three or four hours a day at the least."*

Applying the Insights of our Experts: Good Questions

Let the collective wisdom of our experts help you to conduct an effective job search. Here are key questions from their sage advice for you to consider with each of your job opportunities:

- Can you clearly and confidently share the answer to "why did you leave" or "why were you let go"? Can you explain honestly why you are in the job search?
- Are you allocating most of your time to networking versus responding to online job boards, as networking is the more likely source of finding your next job?
- Are you doing enough homework about each prospective employer and the industry?
- What about the trends in the industry? Do you understand what's going on in the industry?
- Do you understand what each prospective employer is looking for in terms of skills, certifications, abilities, and experience?
- Do you have questions at-the-ready to discuss with prospective employers about topics that are important to you?
- What training could you take right now that would help you become even more marketable?
- If you are about to graduate, is there an internship you could consider that would help you advance your career?
- If you are still in school, do you know your teachers? Do they know you? Have you developed a relationship with them where they can advise you about employers, about your skills? Will they consider offering a recommendation based on what they know about you?
- Do you have a plan to "dig the well before you need water", where you continue your network even after you have been employed?
- How are your online presentation skills? Do you know how to present yourself well in an online interview or networking conversation?
- Do you know enough about the job and prospective employer that you can take the job with confidence? If not, what are you missing?
- If you are unemployed, are you treating the job search as a job and investing a significant amount of time each day advancing your search?
- Are you thanking every person who has been in some way helpful to you?

Good Questions to Ask in a Job Interview:

Our clients often struggle to know what to ask in a job interview. Here is a list to choose from. There would never be enough time to ask them all in any one interview, nor would it be advisable to try. Select the handful you feel you most need to know.

- Why is this job open?
- What are the two or three most important qualifications for success in this position?
- What is the most important contribution you will expect me to make in the first six months? First year?

- What would success for me in this position look like in one year's time?
- What are the issues and problems that need immediate attention in this position?
- Does a job description exist for this position? If so, may I see it?
- What are the most challenging aspects of this position?
- What keeps you at this organization?
- What do you love about working here?
- How many interviews does your company conduct before a decision?
- Tell me three unwritten rules about working in this company.
- What are some of you, and your teams, common frustrations?
- What steps did the company take during the pandemic to keep employees safe?
- How would I be helpful to you personally in this position?
- How would you describe the company's culture?
- Can you tell me about the performance review process?
- Can you tell me about the history of this position in the organization?
- What would be the next career progression from this position?
- Can I meet with other members of the team?
- Does this department have its own budget?
- What are the reporting relationships in this position?
- What is my supervisor's management style?
- How would successful performance be rewarded?
- How is this department/function viewed by others in the company?
- What does it look like during the busiest and toughest times for this role?
- What kind of hours are expected for me to perform the role at maximum capacity?
- Is overtime expected and/or allowed?
- Could you tell me a little bit about the person I would report to directly?
- What is the onboarding process like for new hires?
- What is the turnover rate in this department/company?
- What do you like most about working here?
- What could you tell me about this company that isn't widely known?
- What types of people are most successful here?
- Is there anything I have said or haven't said which would leave you in any doubt that I could do an excellent job for you?
- What would be a reason you wouldn't hire me?

Addendum: Carmela's Proud Tweet Starts a Conversation:

Carmela: "I did it. I asked, "Why should I work for you" in an interview."

Reply from Bill: "At one interview, I brought up (and showed proof) of hundreds of 1-star Glassdoor reviews with the same feedback. I asked them about it, they danced around it, no straight answers. I had a bad feeling, didn't take the job…. Oh, and might I add, that same company when they were closed had their executives charged with tax fraud. I was applying for a senior level role, so I would have been involved. They were looking for scapegoats.... REALLY dodged a big one on that interview."

Reply from Jane, a recruiter: "I love it when someone I'm interviewing starts interviewing me-- it should be a two-way process.

Reply from Winnie: "Good for you! When I was a recruiter, I would have loved to answer that question. I always worked for great companies."

You will find many more questions to ask in the following chapters, organized according to the themes for each of the Lenses.

Lens #3:

Will I Be in for a Shock?

The short tenure rate, or STR, which measures the percentage of jobs that employees leave during their first year of employment, has increased across industries over the past couple of years, according to LinkedIn. The STR started rising dramatically in August of 2021 and continued to rise steadily. LinkedIn labeled the trend "quick quitting."

The rate of quick quitting may have accelerated but leaving a job after only a short tenure is nothing new. In fact, the first few months on the job has always been the period when the most turnover occurs. Here are a few stories from job seekers we interviewed who were shocked by the unexpected in their new jobs and quickly quit:

Teresa: Whole Lotta Shakin'...Not Exactly What She Had in Mind

Teresa was hired as a Marketing Consultant for a brand name cosmetics company but found out quickly that her actual job was to drive around to all the drug stores and shake up the bottles of nail polish, so they'd look fresh. She turned in her resignation after one week.

Miguel Finds Out Money's Not the Main Thing

When the new auto plant opened a few miles away, Miguel heard they were paying much more than he was making as a hotel bellman and shuttle driver at a local world-class hotel. So, he applied and was hired to work as an order picker, pulling auto parts from a wall and placing them in the proper bins for delivery to mechanics. The job required fast, repetitive movement, muscle memory, and he was measured based on speed and accuracy.

On his first day, Miguel was amazed at how fast his trainers were moving compared to his own slow pace. When he asked one of his trainers how long he had been doing the job and was told just a few days, he knew he would never be able to match that pace and learning curve. "I stuck it out for three days, but I really knew on day one that this was not the job for me," he recalls. "I realized quickly how much I was missing the happy people on vacation at the hotel and the beautiful surroundings. Plus, no one day is the same in the hospitality industry." Miguel called his former manager who, thankfully, said he would like to have him back.

Amanda: One-Month as a Flight Attendant

After graduating from high school, Amanda was ready to see the world. She applied to be a flight attendant with a major airline, passed the stringent testing and assessment process, and was hired with flying colors. She is a little embarrassed to admit that she didn't think about the possible drawbacks of a flight attendant's lifestyle before accepting the job. Working with different coworkers every day, adapting to different flight schedules, and staying in a different hotel every night were facts of her new life that she found highly unappealing.

Amanda was forced to realize that what she really needed was a job where she could come home to her own house and belongings every night. And there was never enough time to get out and explore the flight destinations. She was a nester, not a vagabond. And the pay was not enough to put up with the daily ordeal. She was ready to quit after the first paycheck. Another flight attendant that Amanda had told she was going to quit later told her that she could tell by noticing that her knitted brow had become relaxed. Amanda says she would have probably been better suited to be a trainer of other flight attendants at the airline's training center. In fact, Amanda eventually went on to become a very successful corporate trainer. Her advice: "Don't overlook the red flags and hairy warts."

George Finds Wall Street a Little Too Crazy

Fresh out of college, George took an entry-level HR job with a conservative New York City bank. After a few months there, a coworker and friend took a job with an investment firm in the city and encouraged George to follow him there. The friend hired George soon after and George found himself reporting to his friend. But the change in cultures--from the staid and procedural bank culture to wild and disjointed Wall Street--was shocking for George. He also had a hard time relating to the mission of selling pork belly futures. When his friend left the company months later, George was left reporting to a new boss who he described as "a maniac," That was the final straw; George quit that job shortly thereafter. He told us that his intuition told him he was making a mistake when he took the job, but he didn't trust it.

Matt: "Propaganda" vs. The Reality

Matt was impressed. The job posting seemed like a perfect fit for his skills and experience. He reviewed the web site of the prospective employer. There were videos of company leaders touting the great opportunities their company could offer and an "inspiring culture". Matt was looking for certain employee benefits, which were listed on their "careers" page. All looked good.

If Matt had made a few calls or checked out online sites that rated employers, he would have figured out that what was said by the company and what was actually happening were very different. Within a few days it was clear to Matt the culture was definitely not inspirational. It was demoralizing. "I should have done more homework. I would have learned that the image the company was portraying on its website didn't match the reality of working there. In this case, the communication was no more than propaganda."

When the Recruiter is Stumped, it May Be a Bad Sign

Mark's friend thought the interview was going well. Toward the end the recruiter asked him if he had any questions. He had done quite a bit of homework about the company, so he didn't feel a need to ask much on that topic, but he did ask:

"What is the culture like here?"

"Is this a fun place to work?"

"How do team members get along?"

"How often do we meet as a team?"

"What do customers say about the firm?"

Important questions, right? The recruiter couldn't answer ANY of them. Not one. Nada.

Maybe the recruiter was just having a bad day, or MAYBE the performance of the recruiter reflects a company that doesn't know what it stands for and the culture it is building. It could be a very realistic job preview--and a big red flag.

Mark encouraged his friend to network with current and former employees to find out more.

Surveys Reveal Even More Evidence of Shocks and Unmet Expectations

Such stories as these are plentiful and wide-ranging. Here are a few more excerpts from surveys and exit interviews we have done:

"Lots of misinformation was given to me in the interview process. I was never given a plan, as well as other promises that were never fulfilled."

"The job description said this would be a tech support position. I wasn't told I would have to also include billing, returns & exchanges. I also wasn't told about having to stay until the queue was empty each night. These are things I would have thought would be explained upfront to someone applying for this position."

"I did not like the way the trainer made me feel while asking questions about my new job. She made me feel like I was asking 'stupid' questions. I would ask a question and I would be ignored or would get a response with an eye roll or a heavy sigh, not very professional for a trainer, in my opinion."

"I was told when I accepted this management position in another city that when an opportunity came open for a management role in my hometown that I would have the opportunity to transfer back there. After waiting over five years, two management positions became open. However, each time I was passed over for someone else."

**Did the "Great Resignation" Triggered by the Pandemic of 2020-2022
Lead You to Conduct a "Great Reassessment"?**

One result of the pandemic has been individuals re-evaluating what is important to them in their work experience. Many journalists wrote about "The Great Resignation", a term not even in the public domain before 2021.

We hope the "Great Resignation" has moved you to conduct a "Great Reassessment," starting with getting a realistic job preview before taking your next job.

A Reddit user who was starting work as a teacher posted:

"I showed up for work on the first day of school and when I reported to the office to get my classroom assignment/schedule the secretary asked me where my school ID was and what homeroom I was in. I tried to explain to her that I was there to work but she didn't believe me and tried to send me to the principal's office for lying to her."

Amid this ever-changing work environment don't end up in the principal's office.

Find out as much as you can from all available sources.

What the Best Employers Do

We believe you should do all you can to find a job where trust is paramount, and you will be inspired to perform. The first key to doing so is to understand everything you can about the job and organization you are joining.

Many folks are surprised by what they find once they start a new job. They soon realize that the job or the culture is not aligned with what they were told by a prospective employer or what they could ascertain through formal research and insights gained by networking with their contacts.

How important is understanding the job and workplace?

According to survey research conducted by BI WORLDWIDE, newly hired employees are more likely to be engaged at work and stay longer if they agreed with the following statements:

- "I got a good impression of my organization while I was in the hiring process."
- "I learned a lot about my job during the hiring process."
- "I learned a lot about my organization during the hiring process."
- "I got a good impression of my organization while I was in the hiring process."

Can you find people who would willingly refer you to a prospective employer? If you can't, it may say something about the organization. Employees who were referred were more likely to be engaged, committed, working harder, and happier in their jobs than those who were not referred.

Who's Responsible for Realistic Previews: The Employer or the Employee?

The Answer...Both!

Leaders and managers at the best places to work realize that it doesn't pay to portray their jobs and workplaces inaccurately. They know that new hires will soon discover the truth and either leave or become disengaged. Either way, the organization will have lost valuable time and money that they spent hiring, onboarding, and training the new employee. The unrealistic expectations of new hires are the number one cause of short-term turnover. That's why the best employers go to great lengths to make sure that those they hire get a realistic preview of the jobs they fill, the team they will be joining, the working conditions, the potential for career advancement, and the culture.

It is risky for any employer to tell the whole truth because no organization is perfect. There are parts of the job and aspects of every culture that may scare candidates away. The prospect of dealing with angry customers, for example, may scare away candidates for customer service jobs. That's why some companies with the best reputations for customer service make sure that candidates for customer service rep jobs are given the opportunity to listen in on a few calls before accepting a formal offer. Candidates who are put off or scared away by what they hear are better off not taking the job and so is the company. The best-fit candidates for these jobs are those who are not repelled by angry and difficult customers. On the contrary, they are intrigued and attracted by the challenge of empathizing with their complaints, calming them, defusing the situation, and resolving their issues.

Still, many if not most hiring managers are in such a big hurry to fill jobs that they don't take the time or go to the trouble of describing the job or workplace as it really is. So, it is up to you, the job seeker, to get a realistic preview of the job and environment you are about to step into.

Here is a graphic that depicts the "psychological contract" that we all enter when we start a new job. When there is a match between what the employer expects to give and what the employee expects to receive (quadrants 1 and 2), it is likely the *employer* will be satisfied. Likewise, when there is a match between what the employee expects to receive and what the employer expects to give (quadrants 3 and 4), it is likely the *employee* will be satisfied.

The Psychological Contract*

What the Employer expects to Give	What the Employee expects to Receive
1	2
What the Employee expects to Receive	What the Employer expects to Give
3	4

**John Paul Kotter, "The Psychological Contract: Managing the Joining-Up Process," California Management Review, 15 (Spring, 1973): 91-99.*

As you would expect, the more matches of mutual expectations, the more likely it is that you will feel happy and engaged in the job.

With this diagram in mind, look back at your list of the top 20 "Must Haves" you listed in Lens #1. You will be wise to focus on the ones that are most important to you and make sure you find out whether they will be present in your next job. Or you might ask yourself whether you would be willing to trade off one or more of your top preferences for something else you want or need more, such as higher pay or better benefits.

As we have mentioned before, there are always trade-offs in every job because there is no such thing as a perfect job or workplace. But it is better by far to make those trade-offs with open eyes before taking the job than being shocked by the mismatch after starting the job and feeling betrayed or victimized.

Failure to get a realistic preview of the job is the number one reason for turnover during the first six months, when the biggest shocks and surprises normally happen.

Here are some examples of shocking events that can trigger a decision to leave regardless of how long you've been in the job:

- Reporting to a different manager
- Disagreement with manager
- Conflict with a coworker
- Being asked to perform a menial duty
- Being asked to do something unethical
- Realizing you are underpaid compared to others in the same job
- Being pressured to make an unreasonable family/personal sacrifice
- Petty and unreasonable enforcement of authority
- Unexpectedly low performance rating
- No, or low, pay increase
- Being passed over for promotion
- Incident of sexual harassment or racial discrimination
- Close colleague quits or is terminated

A major part of our focus is to help readers who are not happy in their current jobs but are not yet ready to leave their employers. If this describes you, or you have recently experienced a shocking event, we have ideas for how you might be able to become more engaged and decide to stay. We suggest you begin by turning to our Keeping Yourself Engaged chapter and take our *Self-Engagement Survey*. Your results will help you focus on the most personally meaningful of the seven reasons that hold the key to your own job satisfaction and the actions you can take to stay engaged.

A couple more cautionary tales:

Corrine: One Day Was Enough

Corrine was desperate to find a job and took an administrative position in the office of a rendering plant where waste animal tissue is converted into fertilizer and dog food. She was aware of the distasteful aspects of the work in the plant, but she thought that she could stomach being around it if she was confined to the office. However, she could not avoid the smell and seeing and interacting with workers whose aprons were smeared with blood and tissue. She quit after one day and never looked back.

Evan Dismisses the Warning Signs

"I had completed 11 interviews for my dream job with a big title, big team to lead, attractive compensation, with a market-leading company five minutes from my house. I was enthusiastic about the job, but then came a couple of warning signs--my supervisor had seemed a little aloof and in my 12th interview--with the CEO, he didn't impress me.

I accepted the job offer anyway. I was so excited about the job that I overlooked the warning signs and rationalized that I wouldn't be working directly with the CEO anyway. So, I started the job and it immediately felt like a struggle. There had been a lot of lip service about changing the culture and I was looking forward to that challenge. But I soon found out they weren't serious. I started looking for a job within a few months. Looking back on it, I had been talking about that company with friends who had previously worked there. I asked them why they didn't warn me off and they said they didn't want to rain on my parade because I had been so excited about the opportunity."

What Smart Employers Are Doing to Avoid Mismatched Expectations and Disengagement

- Training managers and recruiters to give realistic job previews with every job candidate
- Increasing hiring through employee referrals
- Creating more realistic job descriptions with a short list of critical competencies
- Allowing coworkers to participate in the interview process
- Increasing hiring from within the organization
- Allowing job candidates to sample the actual work experience when possible
- Having new hires complete a post-hire questionnaire

What You Can Do to Avoid Mismatched Expectations and Disengagement

You cannot depend on your target employers to be frank, open, and honest about the less appealing aspects of working there. You will have to do some digging. You will never know everything about what you are getting into, but here are some steps you can take before joining up:

- Review all your work preferences and prioritize the ones you are least willing to trade off (must haves).
- Draft some questions based on your must-have work preferences to ask during A-I-R interviews with "C" contacts. Your "A" and "B" contacts may also happen to know enough about your target employers to respond with insight to your questions as well.
- Read everything you can find about your target employers using their website and *Google alerts* to stay current. Also read comments posted by current and former employees on websites like Glassdoor.com and others.
- Consider proposing a consulting assignment or part-time or temporary position to get experience with the employer before taking a full-time position.
- Always ask for and carefully read the job description for the position.
- Ask everyone who interviews you to describe the workplace culture in 100 words or less. Also ask the same question of former employees, customers, and supply chain partners.
- If appropriate, ask if there is a way to observe current employees performing in the same or similar jobs before taking the job.
- After being on the job and experiencing a shocking or disillusioning event, speak to one or more trusted confidantes to get their thoughts on whether your expectations were unrealistic. If you conclude you were expecting perfection in the workplace, then you must ask yourself whether you can ever accept the distasteful reality for the sake of

keeping the job. The other alternative is to try to change the reality by confronting it or by changing to a different job or part of the organization. When you make a choice and act on it, you are no longer a victim.

Don't Forget to Evaluate the Safety Culture

There was an article in the newspaper about a woman who was invited for an in-person job interview. She thought it went well but didn't get a call back. She followed up and found the position had been filled.

When she asked why they hired someone else, they said: "When you came in for an interview you wore your mask the entire time. We thought you might be one of those people who will complain about every safety issue."

Each of us will need to decide about the kind of work environment where we will feel comfortable working. In the case above, the woman was relieved she found out that their values regarding safety weren't the same as hers and went on to pursue her next career opportunity.

Mark once worked for a utility that highly valued safety, and never felt unsafe when he worked there. That was important to me, so in that case my values and the values of my employer were aligned.

Do your homework. Use online resources and networking to gain insights into the safety culture of a prospective employer.

Is Their Mission Statement Just Wallpaper?

You walk into a company for your job interview. You see a poster, often nicely framed, in the lobby. These statements of the "mission and values" of the organization are often found on their websites as well. They supposedly portray the investments they are making in their employees, customers, and shareholders.

Although they are generally well-intended, it's surprising how often these statements misrepresent what it is like to work there. There is a gap between what they present and what they actually deliver.

As you are considering a potential employer, find out if there's real meaning and substance behind the framed "wallpaper". Talk to former employees, current vendors, or providers of other services to the employer.

No employer is perfect, but if there's a glaring gap between what they espouse and the employee experience they deliver, beware.

Our Panelists Offer Their Perspectives on Avoiding Unhappy Surprises:

Andrea Hendricks: *"Oftentimes individuals take a job out of desperation because they need to get back in the workplace. Desperation predicaments make them take anything. Most job seekers don't look at the culture. You need to come prepared to interview the company. The employer will only give you the sexy stuff. You need to dig deeper! Your job interview isn't the first time you should be seeing the building of a prospective employer."*

Sherry Benjamins: *"Young professionals often have the problem of not having the criteria for how to decide about which job to accept. Plus, they can be easily impressed by the premier consumer brand of a company, not realizing that their brand as an employer may be sadly lacking."*

Ed Baldwin: *"I've stumbled and made some wrong choices in my own career. You know, hiring the right person and choosing the right job are imperfect sciences. The recruitment process is like speed-dating. Things can happen too fast, and employers typically give too little time to filling open positions. You know the old saying, 'Hire fast, suffer slow.' Go to the physical work site. Do they have open cubes or private offices? Ask to speak to the person currently in the position if possible and always speak to your prospective team members."*

Rick Beyer: *"In a job interview, it's important to ask structured questions about the job, characteristics required, and how well aligned it is with your characteristics. The O*Net Online Dictionary of Occupational titles shows personality attributes and competencies required and is a great overall resource. Also read your local city business journal where you will see periodic listings of the top employers in various industries. And don't forget to consider smaller employers with strong potential for growth.   Research your targeted employers by interviewing for information within your network and beyond. Ask people who work there or have worked there what they find appealing. Just remember that no role is perfect. Remind yourself of that going in. If you are already employed, make notes about what you wish you had asked during your job interviews."*

Gary Bolles: *"To avoid being surprised, you must do the homework—get to know the people you will be working with, the problems you'll be taking on, the deliverables that will be expected of you. You also need to do the homework on yourself—taking inventory of your talents, your values, your goals, and everything you need to be happy and successful in your new role. Both you and your next employer are trying to reduce risk. The optimal situation is to be able to kick each other's tires. Before we get married, we reduce risk by dating, but how can we "date" a prospective employer? Taking a consulting role first is like "slow onboarding." Internships and part-time jobs are other ways to reduce risk. Checking Glassdoor still another way. Having access to the previous person who held the job is the center of the target."*

Dennis Boyer: *"When interviewing for a new job, there's a motorcycle analogy that seems apt-- as soon as you start to feel comfortable on a motorcycle, that's when you should feel afraid. You always need to be on high alert when driving a motorcycle. Falling in love with an employer can lead to such laxity and that's when doing the proper homework gets neglected. In my search assignments I've sometimes seen a 'fools-rush-in' phenomenon with both parties--employer and recruit. There can be strong forces that blind both sides when concluding a deal."*

"But both parties should remain cautious--pause and revisit the elements that suggest this is a potential long-term 'marriage'. The search consultant should suggest that; however, equal forces may compel a search consultant to conclude a search assignment without doing so. I'm very proud of completing more than 750 searches in 30 years, achieving many 8–10-year placements, and having only three failed searches. It's good to hit the pause button in these employment discussions."

"Once you're hired, however, be prepared for the possibility that the job you took and the company you joined can become very different later because of profound changes taking place in the industry, the marketplace, or potentially your functional specialty. I've seen this happen so many times. A company's culture can change drastically after going public, experiencing a change in ownership, or hiring a new CEO, for example."

Bill Ellermeyer: *"The job is never going to be what you think it is. There is always going to be something you didn't know that might come as a shock. I once accepted a job that I thought was a generalist HR manager job only to find out it was mainly focused on labor relations and had very little labor relations experience. That didn't work out. Companies should be more upfront about their expectations, but many are still old school and not open or transparent. Sometimes they are afraid you won't take the job if they tell you all about it."*

Mark Ernst: *"Do your due diligence. Look at what current and former employees have to say on Glassdoor.com about your prospective employer. Read the comments carefully. The best employers tend to get mostly good comments. The worst employers do not. If you can, track down people who used to work there through your own contacts and ask about their experience. Listen for what they don't say or if they are guarded in their feedback. Also pay attention to how the organization conducts the interview process. If they are constantly changing interview times, not responding to your calls promptly, or in other ways showing disrespect for you and your time, it says something about their culture. In my experience, that is as good as they're ever going to be."*

Bill Holland: *"There is always a disparity between eating in a restaurant and working in one. It's true of all anticipated work environments. The more you know ahead of time about what will happen, the better because you can anticipate that things will be different from what was expected. You can be better prepared when it happens. That way, you are more aware of the differences between what you might have expected and the realities as they emerge."*

Lynne Nelleman: *"Google www.businessInsider.com and you'll find 55 influential books on best companies to work for and their 'best practices' of business and leadership. Given what you've found out in your research about any potential employers, ask yourself if their practices, senior management, and culture 'fit' you? You'd be amazed at the number of company CEOs who have written books that tell you what is expected of employees."*

"Three other suggestions: One, check TED talks and podcasts for interviews with executives from those companies. Two, follow financial analysts in industries that interest you. Three, you can typically find names of a companies' media or PR staff online or in annual reports. Don't dismiss

information that comes from a company as propaganda. Much of what they have to say is required by law or protocols in certain industries. It must be accurate."

Steve Puente: *"To avoid unhappy surprises when taking a new job, carefully research the employer by going to its website, reading its financials, and learning about its leaders, culture, and mission. Visit the premises and feel the atmosphere. What do you see? Does it feel cheap with old furniture? Are workers jammed together in small offices? Are there wires everywhere? Would you feel embarrassed working there? Ask two critical questions during interviews--'Tell me about your culture' and 'Tell me about the leadership style here.' They should be eager to tell you about both. If they aren't, that's a red flag. Also ask about the employer's orientation process. Good companies do a good job of onboarding new hires."*

Gordon Smith: *"Research the organization as much as possible so you can decide whether you want to interview there in the first place. If you do, then prepare questions to ask. Understand that you are interviewing the employer as much as you are being interviewed and that the interviewer will be judging you on the quality, not the quantity, of the questions you ask. And let the questions you ask demonstrate the homework you have done. If you should end up in a bad-fit situation, don't stay too long, like most people do. I've been in jobs myself where I've stayed too long because I kept hoping things would change for the better, but they never did."*

Applying the Insights of Our Experts: Good Questions

Let the collective wisdom of our experts help you avoid the shock of not having the job fit your initial expectations. Here are key questions from their sage advice for you to consider with each of your job opportunities:

- Are you letting the urgency of needing a job cloud your judgement? What can you do to "slow down" the decision-making so short-term emotions don't lead to a decision you'll regret?
- Have you done enough homework to determine if the "employee brand" -- what's it like to work there-- isn't confused with your interest or affinity for the product?
- Have you visited the location if you will be working on location? Have you met some employees? If so, what are you learning from that experience?
- Have you spoken with former employees, or customers, to see if your impressions are aligned with their experiences?
- Can you summarize what is said about the work experience from public sources such as social media? Are there issues raised on social media platforms that concern you?
- What questions do you have for the prospective employer?
- What have you found out about the prospective employer via interviews, blog posts or podcasts of leaders from that employer?
- Are you "too comfortable on the motorcycle" to the point that you are assuming things you ought not assume about a prospective employer?
- Think carefully about this final question-- what is the one thing you absolutely need to know about the prospective employer for you to continue your conversations with them?

Employers That Know the Value of Giving Realistic Previews

Kansas Child Welfare produced a video on its website showing several of their social workers speaking frankly about both the satisfactions and challenges of the work. They speak frankly about the common perception that they are "snatching babies," but explain that some children must be removed after their investigations confirm that children are found to be abused or neglected. The camera follows them into homes as they describe the angry parents and conditions of poverty they confront in their daily calls.

Wells Fargo Bank requires customer service candidates to watch an interactive video that presents several customer-service-dilemma scenarios. One vignette, for example, shows an angry customer approaching to complain about an incorrect balance; then the video freeze-frames and the job candidate is asked to select from among three possible responses to indicate how he or she would respond. The bank generally eliminates those with the lowest percentage of right answers but also finds that another 20 percent withdraw their applications after viewing the various scenarios that preview the actual on-the-job experience. The company considers this a good outcome, as it eliminates the expense of hiring and training new hires who would eventually quit.

Waste Management created a video that gives driver applicants a realistic glimpse of a driver's 10-12-hour days that start before dawn and are very physically demanding. "If you are not into safety, this job is not for you," says one driver. The video also displays the latest computer technology inside the cab of each truck and emphasizes the importance of teamwork and camaraderie with other drivers.

Applying Insights from Successful Employers:

- Does the prospective employer provide "realistic job preview" content that is in the public domain, such as videos or testimonials from current employees?
- Does this content seem candid and authentic?
- Does the prospective employer provide content that will help you understand the unique situations or challenges you will face in the job? Can you see yourself being successful in those situations?
- Does the prospective employer share the behaviors that are essential to success? If so, can you see yourself embracing those behaviors?

Lens #4:

Will The Job Fit My Talents?

Not all great players can become great coaches.

Marty was an outstanding claims adjustor. He was an attorney by training, and with his previous employer was assigned the most challenging cases. He was admired by his colleagues and had written several articles for industry publications.

He was excited when a competitor asked him to become a manager of a department. He knew the business well and saw this as the next logical step in his career.

Once on the job, it became clear Marty was going to fail in this job. He hated being a manager.

Marty reached out to an old basketball teammate from high school, who was in human resources. After hearing him out, the friend said: "Marty, sometimes people who are great players don't make great coaches. There's no shame in that.

Find a role where you get to use your unique talents and skills."

Marty isn't the only one who has gotten into a role and found that there wasn't a good fit. This is a common mistake job seekers make--taking a job for which there is a poor match between the job and their natural talents, interests, and abilities.

Here are a few quotes from others we've interviewed who also had difficulties with what is often called "person-job fit". Reflect on your own situation as you read them and consider whether you might be putting yourself into a potential job for which this might be the outcome:

> *"After all the training, it still wasn't 'clicking" for me. I just didn't get it as well as I thought I would."*

> *"I felt that my abilities would be better utilized outside of the organization. I felt underutilized and was unhappy with my current work assignment."*

> *"Even after many years in customer service I don't have what it takes to be in sales. I don't feel confident, and I struggle with how to close the sale."*

> *"I was very excited to start this new job as I had never done anything related to this job previously. It was a new field that I was excited about jumping into. It turned out I was not a good fit for the position. I had to do things I wasn't good at doing."*

> *"I felt incompetent in my former job. While interviewing for my new job I got this great feeling of satisfaction when I realized that I was competent in every task expected of me."*

Don't let remarks such as this be your legacy because you didn't find a job for which your skills and abilities were better suited.

Jane Finds the Right Fit

Jane's father worked for a daily newspaper and thought she would make a good reporter, so her father recommended she get a journalism degree. When she was assigned to interview six people on the street as a news writing class assignment, she dreaded the prospect of asking strangers personal questions. She realized then that she hated interviewing people who didn't want to talk to her. Her professor told her, "Jane, you will never make it as a reporter." She reacted with anger. But when she started work as a reporter on a daily paper that summer, she became anxiety ridden. To her chagrin, she was assigned to call and interview the parents of a child who had drowned. She prayed, 'Oh God, please don't let them be at home." She was relieved when there was no answer. The city editor then told her to call the funeral home. Before she could make the call, she was relieved of that duty by the police reporter who did make the call and wrote the story. She lived in fear and dread that entire summer, finally realizing that her news writing professor had been right. The next summer she was assigned to the copy desk, which she loved. She went on to a successful career as a copy editor.

Never Discount the Talents You Use "Just Doing Your Job"

Mark was conducting a workshop with a group of people who had lost their jobs because of a plant closure. They all knew and worked with each other. He had given the group an exercise for each person to think about their successes at work, which can provide insights into strengths (as you have already experienced in the process of listing your achievements and analyzing them to take inventory of your own strengths in Lens #1).

One gentleman in the workshop couldn't think of any successes. His colleagues all jumped in to remind him of several he had. He told the group he "just thought that was what he was supposed to do in his job." Although that may have been true, his friends reminded him he did those things very well! He just hadn't attached the word "success" to them and probably hadn't thought much about what strengths he may have been using.

You may have done some things for so long that you don't realize how special your proven ability could be to another employer. What you've achieved in your prior work (or even in your leisure time) could be proof of the exact talent another employer is looking for, so keep reminding yourself of your successes as you did in Lens #1, even those you may consider modest.

Three ways to recognize your own strengths:

1. Think about when and where you received recognition from others, won an award or contest, received a positive performance review or strong reference letter, or had a "personal best" experience. (Go back and review the Life/Work Achievement Recollection Grid and the Strengths and Talent Inventory you completed in Lens #1).
2. Take time to get feedback from others about your successes. Have friends or former coworkers look at your resume to determine if there's something missing that would be valuable to a future (or your current) employer.
3. Find a way to be more connected to how customers/users experience the results of your work. Are people paying you compliments you never hear?

"How much of me do I get to be at work today?"

Mark has a friend at work with whom he collaborates frequently. They were about to call on a prospective client they had not met. They weren't sure how the meeting would go, but just before the call Mark said, a bit in jest: "Hey, how much of me do I get to bring to the meeting?" His coworker smiled and said: "Bring all of you, Mark!"

Both brought their best that day, and they had a great meeting.
To the degree you can find a place where you can bring *all* of you--your interests, your skills, your passions, and your goals. If the culture of a prospective employer feels like they don't want all of you, the authentic you, it's probably worth taking a pass.

Don't settle. Find a place that will welcome every interest, skill and passion that is you.

What the Research Tells Us About Our Strengths and Staying Engaged

It is important you have a sense that a new job will match your strengths and interests. Research from BI WORLDWIDE emphasizes the importance:

- If a newly hired employee agreed with the statement "When I was looking for jobs, I felt uniquely suited for the position I am in now" they were far more likely to say they were working hard on the part of their employer and bringing their best ideas and creativity to work.
- Forty percent of employees did not agree with this statement! For them the chances of becoming engaged and committed to their employer are lower.
- As you explore whether you "fit", there are three unique elements you should consider—fit with the job, fit with the team and fit with the organization. Each element of fit contributes to the chances you will be happy (engaged) at the job, that you'll get off to a great start and report you are committed to staying with the organization.

Five More Ways to Identify Our Strengths

How can we best determine our "fit" for a role? Dr. Donald O. Clifton was one of the leaders in helping individuals think about how they could effectively apply their strengths in the workplace. He identified a hierarchy of indicators you can use to identify if you have a strength and, importantly, how you could apply it at a prospective employer:

1. First, think about *Yearnings*.
We often have a feeling that "I might like that job"—that's a yearning.
It's a good place to start to search for your talents, so think about those things for which you have yearned when it comes to work (see your "Dream Jobs You May Have Thought Of list in Lens #1).

Although yearnings are a good place to start, we often have yearnings for which we may not have the talent. For example, I LOVE to play golf (a yearning), but I'm awful at golf! In this case my yearning is not an indicator of talent.

The inspirational speaker Orison Marden said: "When we begin to desire a thing, to yearn for it with all our hearts, we begin to establish a relationship with it in proportion to the strength and persistence of our longing and intelligent effort to realize it."

Yearnings are a start. Think about your yearnings, as they may lead you on a journey to the work that would really speak to you.

2. Activities for which you find *Satisfaction*.
So, you thought you might like a job or some part of a job (yearnings), but perhaps you've already done a job or something like it. The next thing you should look for is a sense of satisfaction.

You may still be new to the role and not feel as successful as you would like, but you can still get a sense that you will find satisfaction in the work. Remind yourself again of the times you felt a sense of satisfaction in your work. (Again, review your Life/Work Achievement Recollection Grid in Lens #1, but keep adding to your list as you remember them). Has it been a sustained and recurring feeling or a fleeting one? If the former, you may be onto something.

Although more predictive of talent than yearnings, there are still some tasks that we enjoy but ultimately, we don't become exceptional at them.

3. ***Rapid Learning***.

Have you noticed there are some tasks for which you seem to "catch on quickly"? That could be rapid learning. Have there been new jobs where you were ahead of the training? That could be rapid learning. Have there been jobs where you've helped other new employees who are struggling with tasks you find easy? That was likely rapid learning.

If you're experiencing rapid learning, you're well on your way to finding tasks for which you are optimally suited.

4. ***Glimpses of Excellence***.

This one is even more predictive of success. Dr. Clifton told the story of a track coach, Bob Timmons, who saw potential in a young runner by seeing a short "glimpse" of superior performance. The coach worked with the young runner, helping him build on those glimpses. That runner--Jim Ryan, eventually became a world-record holder.

Often, excellence can be glimpsed at an early age. When George Willig, who climbed the World Trade Center in 1977, was a child, his mother took him to an amusement park. She recalled that he was not that excited about riding on the roller coaster, but he was very interested in how the cars were attached to the tracks. Little George's eye for mechanical detail, already apparent as a boy, was the key to designing the clamps that fit into the window-washing channels of the WTC tower and also made him a very successful toy designer and later, a remodeler of commercial buildings.

There may be times in your past when you've experienced a "glimpse", when you weren't necessarily at peak performance but were showing moments of success. Glimpses can be built upon and nurtured. Those moments can be highly predictive of work where you could be, eventually, very successful.

Want to use your strengths in a new job? Think about the times you have glimpsed yourself achieving exceptional performance, as you did in Lens #1.

5. *Ask yourself whether your **"Total Performance"** Might Have Been Better Than 10,000 People in a Similar Role.* You've heard the expression "one in a million." Dr. Clifton proposed that to be truly exceptional is to be better at something than 10,000 people.

This seems like a provocative and perhaps audacious proposition, but we all have strengths and some of those can be so profound that we can be better than 10,000 people. If you're that good, folks will hire you and reward you well for that talent.

If you have not found your rare talent yet, use the previous four indicators to determine if you're on the right track. If you make it into a role where you are seeing evidence of the first four indicators, you may be on your way.

Louis Pasteur said that *"Genius is one or two talents maximized."* Find those talents, work to develop them, *for they* could make you exceptional.

In summary, use these five indicators to determine if a job offers a potential person-job fit:

- Yearnings
- Satisfactions
- Rapid Learning
- Glimpses
- Total Performance

<table><tr><td>

**Did the "Great Resignation" of 2020-2022 Lead You to Reassess
How You Want to Use Your Talents Differently?**

Let's say you are an excellent performer in your current role, but you have a nagging feeling that the position you currently hold doesn't bring you the same satisfaction it used to bring.

What has changed?

Perhaps you are feeling a need to find a different way to utilize your strengths, one where you feel more satisfaction contributing to a result that feels more aligned with your emerging goals or desires.

For example, the industry in which you find yourself no longer has the same appeal. Or a change in the organizational structure, such as a merger or acquisition, has left you feeling like you are not going in the same direction as the organization.

If you are feeling this, you're not alone. Many of us are anxious about the changes in workplaces today. Use this time to reflect on how you can use what you see as your known strengths and apply them in a role that better fits your goals.

</td></tr></table>

How to Enrich Your Entire Work Experience

Now we focus on some other elements that make the job an engaging, enriching, and satisfying experience, not just with the way your talents match the job, but with a whole set of circumstances.

In 1975 job enrichment researchers Richard Hackman and Greg Oldham conducted a classic study of 658 workers in 62 jobs across seven organizations. Their **Job Characteristics Model** remains a blueprint for job design all these years later. Here are the five elements they identified that must be in place to *achieve employee satisfaction:*

1. <u>Skill Variety:</u> **Will you use the mix of skills and talents that you most want to use?** Look again at the talents you prioritized in Lens #1. Will your next job make use of this particular mix of talents? If you are currently employed and not using the talents you most enjoy, here are some actions you can take:

- Seek a better match of your talents to the work that needs doing.
- Look for a new task or project.
- Avoid overloading yourself with too many responsibilities or duties.
- Swap some job tasks with another team member.
- Find ways to use your underused talents in your leisure time.

2. <u>Task Completion:</u> **Will you be allowed to complete an identifiable piece of work from beginning to end with a visible outcome?** Most of us feel that it is more meaningful and satisfying to complete a larger task or project than to be limited to smaller tasks. To enrich your job on this criterion:

- Look for ways to complete more steps in the work process.
- Try to get in position to observe the outcome of the task.
- Seek responsibility for managing a project from beginning to end.

3. <u>Task Significance:</u> **Does the job have a recognizable positive impact on the overall mission, on customers, on users or on other team members?** If your job or your prospective job falls short on this criterion, you can pursue these options:

- Ask until you fully understand why the job is vital to the organization and its mission.
- Learn how doing the job well positively impacts customers/users and coworkers.
- Consider moving into a job that feels more significant or meaningful to you.

4. <u>Autonomy:</u> **Does the job offer substantial freedom, independence, and discretion in planning how the work will be done?** If not, think seriously about these options:

- Communicate your ideas for improving how the job or task is done.
- Ask for more freedom to make decisions.
- Ask your manager to delegate (offload) more tasks to you.
- If possible and allowable, request that your performance evaluation be based more on results achieved instead of on whether you followed a prescribed work process.

5. <u>Feedback</u>: Do you get to see progress and results of your work and the impact on customers, users, and coworkers? We address actions you can take to get more and better feedback in the next chapter. These options may work for you:

- Seek to redesign the job so you're allowed to see for yourself the impact you are having.
- Ask for more coaching and more frequent feedback.

Our Panelists Share Their Wisdom on Job-Person Fit

Ed Baldwin: *"Speaking as someone who has written them, job descriptions stink. So always ask what percentage of time you'll be spending on which important activities. Ask the current jobholder about a typical day. Where do they spend the most and least energy? What is the one thing most needed for success?"*

Sherry Benjamins: *"Getting hired is not just about your collected experience. In today's job market it's about knowing the organization and how your strengths can make a difference in the business. You must reinvent yourself to keep up with the pace of change."*
"As an executive search consultant, I have been frustrated for years by clients who present me with a list of 15 requirements for a position they want filled, giving all 15 equal importance. Instead of focusing on the few essential talents, they are looking for an ideal that doesn't exist in all too many cases. Both interviewer and candidate need to be better skilled at talking about what success looks like, not just a list of 15 requirements."

"When hiring younger professionals, employers need to focus on proven ways of evaluating life experience and potential, not performance, since their work experience is limited. This is especially true for most diversity candidates. They need to be developed, not trained. They want to be honest in job interviews, but they feel they will disqualify themselves by admitting they don't know something. Too many employers have a replacement mentality instead of a mindset of investing in their employees."

Rick Beyer: *"Finding our best fit in the workplace starts with knowing ourselves--our skills, aptitudes, and personality. The Big Five Personality Assessment (which measures Emotional stability, Extraversion, Agreeableness, Conscientiousness, and Openness to experience), The Holland Self-Directed Search Survey, the Strong Interest Inventory, and the Hogan Assessment are all helpful."*

"If, after starting a job, evidence of a mismatch exists, coaching often improves fit by enabling an employee to leverage bright-side personality characteristics, dampen the manifestation of dark-side attributes, and build on motives, values, preferences, and interests. Further, it is often possible to engage in job sculpting or enrichment to design jobs to better match the characteristics of those who perform the jobs. Organizations can influence skill variety, task

completion, task significance, autonomy, and feedback in ways that improve your self-motivation, work satisfaction, engagement, performance, commitment, and retention."

Gary Bolles: *"Self-inventory is the place to start. Be clear about what you want to do and where you want to do it. Then you need to need to know how to research the job well enough to find out if it fits your requirements based on your self-inventory. Before you sign the acceptance agreement, be clear about what your work role will be. Hiring should be a team sport, so for the sake of teamwork everyone on your future team should have a say and buy in to what your role will be. Be warned that things can change after you take the job. A reorganization could change everything. Or a mismatch can develop over time."*

Dennis Boyer: *"Job candidates have lots of questions but are typically reluctant to ask too many questions because they want to appear informed, and they don't want to appear difficult. But it's not unreasonable to ask what the job entails day-to-day. I advise candidates to ask about specific job tasks and expectations. If you can talk to the previous holder of that job, ask what kept them up at night. Track down that person if you can and probe a little bit. There's usually something about the job that they didn't discover in the recruiting process and that became a surprise. You can avoid such surprises by sourcing people who have been there before and by drilling down a bit ahead of time."*

Mark Ernst: *"Matching yourself to the job is important but match yourself to the culture first. Trust your instincts if it doesn't feel right. If you're over 50 and you see no one over 30 during the interview process, you must ask why there are no senior people there. Is it because they actively discriminate against older candidates? If you learn that everyone you meet during interviews has only been there two years or less, you must wonder if they have a "burn-and-churn" culture. When you interview or go to the job site ask yourself: do people look happy and engaged, or are they harried, running around as if everyone has their hair on fire. That should be a strong warning sign."*

Bill Ellermeyer: *"A big part of the problem is the lack of good job descriptions, especially in small companies. Even large companies don't do a good job of defining jobs. As a result, they often hire someone too powerful for the job or not powerful enough. I coached an executive who went to work for a $70 million aerospace company that had never documented procedures or job duties in writing. When you start a new job, always ask to speak to the current or previous person in the job if possible. Ask them about the kinds of issues and problems they face, what skills are needed, and what results are expected."*

Andrea Hendricks: *"The job description is just a guide. But if you take it as literal, you will be shocked how different it is from the actual job. We must encourage talent to find ways to think about fit in a broader sense--what talents do I bring that can help with emerging needs? Where can I contribute? These are the questions job seekers need to ask. You also must be ready when a job changes that you initially thought was a good fit. This happened when the CEO hired me and then left."*

Lynne Nelleman: *"Hiring personnel and managers are sometimes pushed to hire 'warm bodies' just to fill job openings, especially as we saw in the post-Covid 19 rush to gear up quickly and get back in business. It's a quantum leap from a warm body to the right person, in the right place, at the right time."*

"I take a small pad of paper with me into discussions about a job or new position, asking "do you mind if I take notes?" Never had a person say 'no.' Rather, they were flattered that I felt their input SO important. With this approach you (1) indicate you're serious, (2) buy time saying you'd like to get back to them after you've reviewed your notes, (3) can ask to have a short conversation with a person in the company who holds the position, and (4) in a 'thank you' letter for the interview or offer--suggest additional responsibilities and compensation."

Steve Puente: *"Read the job description carefully to determine exactly what you will be asked to do. At the same time, don't assume the job description is up to date or fully descriptive of what your critical communication objectives will be after you've taken the job. Ask what results they expect you to have achieved in the first 12 months. By all means don't fake it and sell yourself into a job that doesn't match your strengths. Try to network and go on LinkedIn to find people who worked there. Approach them to get their perspective on the company."*

Gordon Smith: *"I believe that when you see a job of interest described in an ad or listing, draft a type of cover letter known as a "T-Letter" -- basically a bulleted listing of "Your Requirements" on the left and "My Qualifications" on the right to clearly show the corresponding matches. You may realize in the process that you don't have the qualifications needed or that you are overqualified. Your cover letter may never be read, but the process of writing it will be valuable even if you never send it.*

"I also recommend candidates use Jobscan.co (not .com) which will help you measure the percentage of matches using their system based on key words. If there is not at least a 70% match, you may be risking getting hired into the wrong job. Some employers will have you complete a pre-employment questionnaire or assessment. Answer the questions honestly. Don't try to fake it and answer them the way you think they would like. Imagine getting the job and having to pretend you are somebody else five days a week, 52 weeks a year."

"Also, keep in mind that many employers are using pre-pandemic job descriptions that are outdated. And remember--bosses' expectations are often different from the job description. I advise candidates to ask prospective employers this question: 'If you and I were sitting down six months from now and you were telling me what a great job I was doing, what would you say I had accomplished?'"

Applying Insights from Our Experts-- Good Questions

Let the collective wisdom of our experts help you identify opportunities where job-person fit is in evidence. Here are key questions from their sage advice for you to consider with each of your job opportunities:

- How will you spend most of your time in your new role, and will you likely use your best and most satisfying talents in those activities?

- Can you easily see how you will connect your strengths--what you do well--to the mission and future growth of the organization?
- Will you get coaching and feedback about how you can develop your strengths in this opportunity?
- Do the people with whom you interview at a prospective employer seem to be in roles where they are using their strengths?
- Do you see ways to use your strengths to help the organization pursue previously unrecognized opportunities or gain competitive advantage?
- Does your potential hiring manager express an understanding of your strengths as you get into the interviewing process? Do you think the hiring manager is in a role that fits his or her strengths?
- As you gain a better understanding of the results the organization is trying to achieve, can you see yourself making a difference in those results in your first year there by leveraging your strengths?

Employers That Excel at Matching Job and Person

Are there companies who see the value of job-person fit? You bet. Here are three organizations whose commitment to this lens is clear. Take inspiration from these employers as you evaluate this lens for each job opportunity:

Weiser Security gives all security guard candidates a 100-question assessment to slot them into one of four best-fit roles and work settings most suitable for their personalities: Greeters (for lobby and information desk roles), Gratifiers (for more service-focused roles, as in airport pre-board screeners), Graveyarders (those more comfortable with solitary assignments, such as night watch roles), and Grinders (who generally perform closed-circuit monitoring or multi-tasking assignments). The Gallup Organization scored the company 89 percent better than other organizations at finding the right person for the job.

At **Whole Foods Markets**, teams, and only teams, have the power to approve new hires for full-time jobs. Store leaders screen candidates, then recommend them for jobs on a specific team. After the team interviews the candidate, a two-thirds vote is required for a hire. Then the candidate doesn't become a permanent employee until after a 30-day trial period. Teams routinely reject new hires before 30 days are up if they turn out not to have the right stuff. Not everyone fits the Whole Foods profile--people who are "serious about food, have a knack for pleasing customers, and can tolerate the candid give-and-take that's necessary for a workplace democracy." Another reason that Whole Foods team members are so tough on new hires is that the company's gainsharing program ties directly to team performance. If team members vote for someone who doesn't perform, their bonuses will be less.

Rackspace, a leading information technology hosting company, is passionate about helping its employees find their strengths and describes its culture as "strength-based." New hires receive a strength assessment and attend a two-hour class on strengths. The company's leaders expect managers not to hoard their talent. If an employee ever gets into a role that under-utilizes his or her top strengths, managers are expected to allow the individual to explore roles that might be a better fit.

Applying Insights from Successful Employers-- Good Questions

As you're exploring a potential employer, ask yourself these questions:

- Does the prospective employer have a method for understanding the strengths of each candidate? Is the process, as far as you can tell, fair and equitable for all candidates?
- Do they use validated candidate "success profiles," "personas" or some other way to determine the candidates who are likely to be most successful in a role?
- What role, if any, do other team members have in who gets hired? Can you talk with them prior to being hired to discuss what they view as the strengths that will help someone who is hired be successful?
- Does the prospective employer have resources in place to help you learn more about your strengths and how they can be applied if you are hired?
- Does the culture of the organization allow you to seek other positions for which you can use your strengths and, in doing so, make even greater contributions?

Looking For Fit in Each Job Opportunity-- The Job Fit Grid

For years we've coached job seekers to use the following tool to evaluate a specific role and determine whether there is sufficient evidence of job-person fit.

The exercise is quite simple. Look at all the information you've collected for a specific job. This information will come from sources such as a job description, but you'll also need to collect insights about a job from contacts you've made and insights they've provided.

Here is an example of a completed grid from "Bill," who successfully applied for and was accepted into a job at an academic medical lab for which he now has confirmed a strong job-person fit.

Key Skills and Strengths Required	How do I fit?
Degree in genetics	Just received a degree in genetics.
Specific experience in a lab.	Two years of experience in a lab. Enjoyed the job, which gave me evidence of **satisfaction** for the role. I excelled quickly in the lab (evidence of **rapid learning**).
Presentation skills.	Received awards for presentations in academic training as well as work in the lab. Received prizes for presentations I made outside of academic training, (**glimpses** of outstanding performance).
Collaboration skills.	In previous jobs I enjoyed working with a larger team at the lab. I preferred this work to being a more independent lab worker (strong evidence of **satisfaction**).

Use this job-person grid to evaluate each job opportunity. Find evidence that the role has strong job-person fit.

Do you feel you have the information you need? If so, proceed to complete this form:

Key Skills and Strengths Required	How do I fit?

Completing this simple exercise can significantly increase your chances of finding and maintaining a satisfying job.

Telling The Story of Your Strengths

Now that you've gained a deeper understanding of your strengths, you'll need to be prepared to communicate those strengths to prospective employers. We recommend using the "SARL" model:

- Tell about a **situation** where you were challenged to be at your best and use your strengths,
- Explain, in detail, the **actions** you took to meet the challenge,
- Provide the **results**, in as tangible way as possible, of how you addressed and the challenged, and
- Share what you **learned** from this situation that might help you address future problems.

You will first want to review your successes, which you've documented based on the inventories in Lens #1. Take four or five of your successes and prepare for the inevitable question you'll get in a networking conversation or job interview…

"Tell me about a time when…"

These questions can be difficult but preparing a SARL for several of your strengths will put yourself in the best position to effectively communicate your strengths. Being able to communicate your strengths will differentiate you in a competitive market. Here's an example:

Question	Your Response (Proof of Talent)
Tell me about a time when you turned a project from what looked like a failure and made it into a success.	*I came into a branch of our business. The current manager was not producing results and was asked to leave. The manager role was offered to me. I gathered our team and we talked about our situation. We knew we couldn't predict what our sales would be, so we didn't worry about that. We identified the things we could do to impact sales for which we had control. The more we identified things we could do the more excited the team got. We*

	met weekly and discussed our successes and how we could build on them. We also identified gaps in our customer service and what we could do to improve. After three short months we turned the branch profitable. I learned that if you focus on what you can control and inspire your team to meet goals that you can achieve a lot.
Describe a time when you identified a problem and came up with a solution before others.	*I was working in the employee relations department of an insurance company. I saw a trend of certain cases that had, in my opinion, a pattern. The pattern indicated that the management of a business group didn't understand they were telling employees to do things that weren't in compliance. I looked back at hundreds of prior cases to see if this pattern had appeared before. What was clear is that new regulations were being interpreted differently. There were gaps in our leaders' understanding of these new rules. I recommended communication of these new regulations and training to minimize them being broken again. I received a commendation from my two-up manager for seeing the trend before it became a bigger problem. I learned that seeing these trends and doing my homework to verify them can help our business maintain its compliance.*

Your strengths deserve a workplace where they can be used and in a role for which you find meaning and satisfaction. Learn how to communicate what you do well and its value to the organization.

Lens #5:

Will I Get the Feedback and Coaching I Need?

"I love being coached. I get angry when I'm not coached. I ask a lot of questions and certainly appreciate any insight and feedback. I think if you ever stop listening to coaching or stop asking questions, you probably need to be doing something else."

–NFL Hall of Famer, Peyton Manning

Viv's story: The line between empowerment and abandonment

Viv prided herself on being able to tackle problems and find ways to solve them. The recruiter who hired Viv noted that her problem-solving skills were mentioned by two of her references.

But when Viv started the new job, it was clear that she was going to be "thrown to the wolves", receiving little onboarding and even less support from a manager. In the case of the manager, she seemed like a good person, but was so busy fighting other fires that she had little time for Viv.

Six months into the job Viv received a formal appraisal from her manager, who brought up several problems regarding her work. One of them was with a project Viv had worked on in her first month. As her manager was describing the problem Viv realized what she had done wrong but getting the coaching several months later wasn't helpful.

By that time Viv knew her chances of redeeming herself in the eyes of her manager weren't good, so she polished up her resume and started a confidential job search.

"I would have been happy to take the feedback and make changes in how I approached the work, but by the time my manager got around to telling me, it felt like it was too late. I want a work environment where I am empowered to do my job, but in this case, I felt more abandoned than empowered."

Management Skills That Are Sadly Lacking

A survey of 1,149 workers at seventy-nine different companies found that manager feedback and coaching skills were consistently rated as mediocre. *

It should not be surprising that coaching and managing the performance of direct reports are skills that do not come naturally to most managers. And chances are, your next manager has not been properly trained in basic principles of performance management, coaching, and giving feedback.

Here are the comments from exiting employees (at different employers) who left because of the lack of effective coaching and timely feedback:

'"Managers tell you everything you do wrong and nothing you do right.

"The worst part of my new job was feeling completely lost and not doing things correctly at first.

"The manager was unwilling to work with me to learn work procedures. She also humiliated me in front of a coworker. She never had anything positive to say to me.

"My manager never showed a little compassion or made a true attempt at trying to learn my needs or concerns to assist me with being the best employee I could be.

"My current manager spends more time watching football games, keeping an eye on his fantasy team, and sitting around than he does training, working the phones, sending emails, or cleaning. He does not lead by example.

"The company bends over backward to keep employees who are performing below average.

"The leadership team does not trust employees to do the work they were hired to do. The amount of oversight and scrutiny of our day-to-day work leaves us feeling as though we are not trusted to make decisions that would be in the best interest of the customer and the company. Ideally, our leadership team would provide the strategy and guidance--pointing us in the right direction--and let us do our best work within those guard rails.

"If managers would just stop micromanaging every single little thing and let the people who go out and do the work that they deal with on a day-to-day basis, things would be a lot easier for both the company and the employees."

"The way that 'group punishment' methods are frequently used - i.e., one person clearly causes an issue, but the entire group is called out as if everyone had performed the action."

These comments testify to the general lack of competence in this key skill. Many managers are not even paying attention to the people they supervise. As many managers have said to their direct reports, "If you don't hear from me, it means you're doing a good job." The problem is that it usually doesn't mean that at all. In some organizations, giving feedback on performance is occurring irregularly or not at all. At other employers, basic expectations and changes in work procedures are not being communicated. Employees who fail to perform up to standard are not being confronted. Managers are allowing themselves to be influenced by politics and favoritism. And last, but certainly not least, many employees are hesitant to ask for feedback when they need it.

What the Research Shows:

We want to perform well, and it is critical we receive candid, meaningful feedback from those with whom we work. According to research from BI WORLDWIDE:

- Managers are a critical source of feedback. Sadly, one in four employees don't feel well understood by the manager.
- When employees feel understood, they are happier on the job and more inclined to perform at a higher level for the enterprise.
- Ninety-one percent of employees whose managers understand them are happy with their current jobs, and those who are happy are nine times more likely to be performing with greater intensity.
- Employees who feel understood are far more likely to recommend their organization as a great place to work and more likely to say working there brings out their best ideas.
- Women and those with less than a bachelor's degree, on average, perceive lower levels of being appreciated for their strengths in their jobs. Having just one of these risk factors--being a woman, starting a job over age 45, or having less than a bachelor's degree, results in being half as likely to feel understood as an individual. Those with all three risk factors are eight times less likely to feel understood than those with none.
- Thirty percent of employees say they don't meet regularly with their manager, making it more difficult to be understood.

**Did the "Great Resignation" of 2020-2022 Lead You
To Reassess Your Expectations of Your Manager?**

In today's changing work climate you may be feeling the need for additional support and insights from your manager:

For example, with more of us going to a "hybrid" or "remote" workplace, you may find yourself considering a new role where you may not have the same contact with your team and supervisor, which even without intent may lead to fewer opportunities to receive ongoing coaching and feedback.

In this new work environment, do your homework so you don't feel in a vacuum when it comes to the support you need.

Why Managers Don't Provide Coaching and Feedback:

- Many managers fear or dread the prospect of hurting, offending, arguing with, alienating an employee, or even losing control of their emotions when giving difficult feedback.
- They are so busy with their own projects that they don't feel they have time to observe and track employees' progress.
- They feel they will fail because of their lack of training.
- The sheer number of meetings, virtual and otherwise, plus travel and client interactions make it harder to give timely feedback.
- They never received skilled or positive coaching themselves.
- They have a fundamental dislike for or bias against an employee under their supervision (see Appendix A on dealing with bias).

Perhaps you have had such poor coaching and feedback with a previous manager that it has put you on alert to avoid a similar such experience again. Or perhaps you have had a manager who gave you excellent feedback and coaching and you want to get more of the same in your next position.

Either way, you need to know how much coaching and feedback *you* want and need. Look back at your list of key "Must Have" preferences in Lens #1. If you listed anything related to coaching and feedback as a strong need or desire in your next job, this is an important chapter for you.

Sharon's Boss Forgets to Tell Her His Expectations

To supplement her husband's income while he was in the Army, Sharon took a job as a Loss Prevention Operative, working to catch and arrest shoplifters for a major department store. She liked the idea of bringing wrongdoers to justice, but she didn't like having to chase after the *ones who resisted or tried to run away. But she persisted in the job until two events converged. First, her supervisor told her she wasn't meeting her quota of arrests <u>after never telling her there were quotas to be met in the first place.</u> Then, after catching the intoxicated wife of an Army officer shoplifting, the officer threatened to have Sharon's husband transferred to a war zone. That's when she decided to quit the job. She found out later that when the news about his wife came out, the Army officer had himself been sent to the war zone.*

Why We Need Feedback and Coaching

We need timely feedback and coaching to help us answer four basic questions:

1. What are the goals of the team and organization?
2. What is the plan for getting there?
3. How am I expected to contribute?
4. How am I doing?

The right time to get answers to the first three questions is during the interview process before taking the job. Getting clear answers to these three questions will help get you off to a good start.

The graphic below shows the radical difference between the traditional way managers have coached employees for years and the "Partnering" model that involves the employee in the performance planning process and makes it a continuous process instead of a once-a-year event. In recent years large employers such as Microsoft, Accenture, Cigna, Deloitte, and Medtronic have abandoned or overhauled the traditional model in favor of the Partnering model. Will your next employer be one of those that has trained its managers in how to partner with employees in performance planning, continuous coaching, and feedback? Or not?

Performance Coaching Models
Traditional vs. *Partnering*

Traditional	Partnering
• Manager-driven	• *Employee has input*
• Parent-to-child	• *Adult-to-adult*
• HR exercise	• *Manager's tool*
• Personality	• *Results*
• Vague goals	• *Specific objectives*
• Yearly event	• *On-going*
Gets Compliance	**Gets <u>Commitment</u>**

Questions to Ask Before Joining Up

Here are some other questions you may want to ask in the job interview with your manager or with other team members in the organization:

- How often can I expect to receive feedback on my performance?
- Do you welcome employees taking the initiative and requesting feedback when needed?
- What specific results do you expect me to achieve in the first six months and first year? (Another way to ask is, "What does success look like in this job?")
- Has the job description changed recently for any reason?
- Do you have an updated copy of the job description that I can see?
- Will my performance goals be updated throughout the year?
- How often will I receive a formal performance review?
- Will I be encouraged to track my own progress and write my own performance goals and reviews?
- How closely will my performance measures be linked to pay increases?

Jack: Loved the Work, But the Boss...Not So Much

After retiring from the Army, Jack transitioned into a project manager position for a manufacturing company. After a few years he was ready to move on from that role. He was hired for a position at a nearby university that paid significantly better. The job involved managing the administrative details and budget at a large research center. Jack thought it was a good fit because he had management experience, had taught in a university setting, and had a degree in a related technical field. He would be taking care of the "administrivia" that academics were all-too ready to offload.

The work was fascinating, and Jack performed well, but he and his boss were not a good match. The boss always needed to be in the spotlight and had trouble sharing credit. He pouted, avoided conflict, and went on long, rambling rants when Jack made decisions he didn't like. Jack endured the situation for three years because the work was interesting and important, and he was proud of what he was accomplishing in the job. He finally resigned on a day when he realized he was starting to buy into the boss' view of him. Jack wishes he had done more due diligence--inquiring about the boss' management style from people he knew before accepting the position. He faults himself for being too anxious to leave his previous position and too focused on getting the pay increase.

Which of The Four Types Will Your Next Manager Be?

Regardless of what kind of performance coaching model your next or current employer endorses and practices, we all want to work for a manager who generally treats people right.

The diagram below illustrates four types of managers, with type 1 representing the "ideal boss'--one who has enough empathy and concern to treat employees right while also achieving the desired business results ("making the numbers"). Type 2 managers may have good instincts about people but may need more coaching or experience to become effective at getting the desired results.

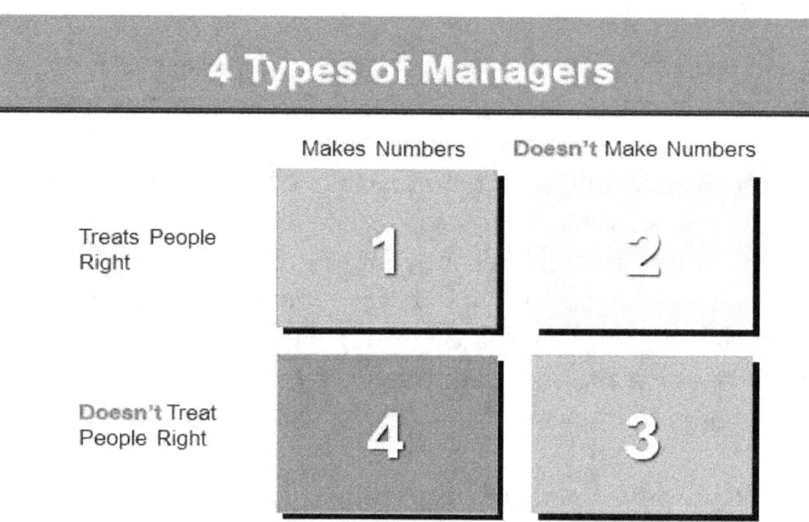

Type 3 managers lack both the human touch and the necessary focus on results and may need to be prevented from holding jobs requiring supervision of others or removed from their people management roles altogether. Type 4 managers are more problematic for senior leaders. Do they keep managers in place who abuse their employees but still manage to get results? All too often, the answer is yes. In the long run those kinds of managers do more harm than good, driving away the talent they need to sustain their success. When the war for talent is intense, Type 4 managers become more difficult to tolerate.

Our wish for you is that you get to work for a Type 1 manager who is not only more likely to give you better coaching and feedback but is also less likely to give you cause for leaving for any of the reasons outlined in the next few chapters.

Ashley Finds Out Her Friend is a Not-So-Friendly Boss

Ashley was furloughed from her inside sales job during the pandemic and began looking for a job immediately from her home office. After two months, she was feeling desperate to pay bills, but was fortunate enough to reconnect with a former coworker and friend who hired her as a sales manager at a growing medium-size company. Ashley had fond memories of working alongside her new boss in their previous job, but she realized quickly after starting in the new job, that working for him was going to be a very different experience.

"He was micromanaging me from day one, constantly hovering and checking on my work to the point of obsession. The day he yelled at me for overlooking the smallest detail, I couldn't sleep that night. I resigned the next day. It was sad to lose a job and a friend on the same day, but I

was relieved to be out of there and don't regret leaving. Before taking my next job, I made sure to talk to my future coworkers about the boss' management style.

Getting the Feedback and Coaching You Need *After* Joining Up:

You may be seeking a "frequent feedback culture"--an organization where every day there are informal, frank, spontaneous, free-flowing performance reviews going on--in the lunchroom, the hallways, and in every business meeting. Such cultures are all-too-rare, unfortunately, but they do exist. But here are some ways to get the coaching and feedback you need even if you don't work for such an employer:

- Whenever you believe you are not receiving the feedback and coaching you need, ask your manager to meet with you to discuss how you can improve your performance. If you have just started your job, ask for a feedback discussion at 30 and 90 days.
- Prepare yourself by Googling and reading articles on how to receive feedback.
- Develop the habit of asking for feedback from peers, customers, direct reports, coworkers on team projects and task forces, and anyone with whom you might interact, not just the boss. Consider seeking out an informal mentor. As a wise person once said, "Feedback is the breakfast of champions."
- If you receive feedback that is too general or too difficult to understand, ask for specific examples.
- If you have never been invited to write your own performance objectives or give your own self-evaluation, ask your manager to let you do so.
- If you are not comfortable with your performance objectives or performance appraisal results, speak up. Try to reach a satisfactory mutual understanding with your supervisor.
- If you feel that changes in circumstances require that changes be made in your performance objectives, request a meeting with your supervisor to rewrite the objectives.
- If the employer makes 360 feedback assessments available, consider asking if you are eligible to participate in receiving feedback from third-party peers and even from the customers you serve.
- If you feel you are spending more time trying to improve weaknesses than building on your strengths, change your developmental objectives, your manager, or your job.
- If the organization retains external coaches to assist current employees, ask if such coaching is available at your position level. If not available, consider retaining an outside coach of your own.
- If you work for a manager who is not coaching you or giving the feedback you need, consider seeking a new position within the company where you can work for a different manager, or pursue employment elsewhere.

Our Panelists Share Their Insights on Coaching and Feedback:

Renny Arensberg: *"At KVC Healthcare thirty percent of our managers' performance rating is based on how well they develop individuals and teams. Program leadership sets clear goals that individuals and teams are expected to accomplish. Essential tasks and the performance standards for tasks are made clear to optimize quality of work. Leadership holds individuals and teams accountable to their goals and performance standards through monitoring, praise, recognition, and feedback. Leadership provides an opportunity for individuals and teams to reflect on and enhance their workplace experience through action planning."*

"We explore the unique contribution of every individual to enhance self-awareness and understanding of others. Opportunities are provided to develop innate skill and manage areas of weakness. Team leadership establishes the culture of the team through setting the tone, pace, and environment. All teams are expected to honor diversity, strive for inclusion, prioritize relationships, and have fun. I would advise all job seekers to look for an employer that takes employee coaching and development as seriously as we do."

Ed Baldwin: *"Ask your future boss how they have handled direct reports who didn't perform. Does the boss' response reassure you that he/she values giving honest, two-way, constructive feedback and coaching?"*

Sherry Benjamins: *"There is a huge cry for feedback from early career professionals or Millennials. One of my mentees reported that she had no one-on-one meetings with her boss for six months. I suggested she approach the boss with a partnership agreement based on shared goals, aspirations, actions to take, and how they see shared accountability. I counsel young people to take the initiative for their own learning and getting feedback. Two of my learning group members (I call them "learners") recently followed that advice and have been promoted or had their roles expanded."*

Rick Beyer: *"We all want rich and specific feedback. So, try to find out if the culture and your future manager are known for giving it. How does their performance management system and process work? Are 360 assessments available? Will I be able to have two-way conversations with my boss? Will there be regular check-ins? Will I get to weigh in on my goals? Will my manager help me see clearly how my job helps the company succeed?"*

"After you're hired, ask for feedback if it isn't optimal. Ask coworkers and customers for feedback if you're not getting it from the boss. Get it from the job itself. Some people have asked for a 360 assessment and gotten it. Others have requested and received coaching from outside consultants."

Gary Bolles: *"My belief is that we need to move from the model of managers being "the sage on the stage" to being "the guide on the side." I prefer the term "team guide" instead of "manager." The team guide's job should be to coach the team members, support them, and* *build a culture where everyone is comfortable giving honest feedback to each other. Most organizations don't teach managers how to play that role. In your research and questioning before taking the job, you can ask how team guides are trained to conduct ongoing discussions. Also ask if the training is available to everyone who might lead a project and whether every single worker has access to internal mentors and external coaches."*

Dennis Boyer: *"When I was at Marriott Hotels managers were required to have weekly coaching sessions with their direct reports. We called them 'ping-pong sessions' because there was always back-and-forth discussion, and the employee had a voice. We were encouraged to be constantly developing talent and to be in touch with the employee's career goals. But many companies are poor at this. Giving feedback requires candor and confrontation. Many bosses don't have the time, the inclination, or the capability. It feels uncomfortable."*

"So, employees sometimes need to do their share to fill that void. Employees should take partial responsibility and initiate discussion about constructive feedback, even coax or coach the boss if necessary. Learn about coaching and feedback best practices. You can help make your boss more successful and reap benefits in your own career. During the job interview you can also ask the manager for an example of a former direct report who was successful or one who failed-- what were the factors involved? You can ask about the company's specific expectations of managers in terms of coaching and about the performance review process."

Bill Ellermeyer: *"It's rare to get a thorough performance review and the idea of getting only one per year is absurd. Ideally, you will have a mentor relationship with your boss, but that is all too rare. Managers in fast-paced companies are incredibly busy and are usually not held accountable for coaching their direct reports. They need to make it comfortable for the people on their team to ask for feedback. Millennials especially want to know why they are doing what they do and how the boss thinks they are doing."*

Mark Ernst: *"Ask about their formal performance review process. But even more importantly, find out the company's policy about manager coaching and feedback. The best employers hold managers accountable for conducting performance check-ins with their staff at least every other week. Ask how frequently your manager will meet with you to discuss your performance. It should be at least weekly during your first 90 days. Also, will your manager reinforce your strengths during these meetings or just criticize what you've done wrong. Feedback that says you're doing a good job is the best kind of feedback. Bias may be an issue with some managers. A former employee might have the best insights about that."*

Andrea Hendricks: *"Employers need to have mentoring programs available. Leadership development programs need to be in place. Companies who have that will receive greater levels of engagement. These programs should be both formal and informal. Even executives still need it."*

Bill Holland: "*Simply ask your interviewers 'Would you consider your workplace to be a low, medium, or high feedback environment?' Then ask, 'How so?' Pepsico at one time, for example, considered itself a low feedback environment. They would say that right up front. By contrast, IBM has always prided itself on giving employees regular formal feedback opportunities. It is a* *matter of knowing what kind of environment you work best in. The important thing in any work culture is to know exactly what is expected of you and get as close to achieving those results as you possibly can."*

Anne Maltese: *"In our research at Quantum Workplace we are finding that remote coaching can work well when employee goals are captured and well documented in software. This raises the visibility of those goals for the manager and for the employee. Companies that are serious about managing performance and goal setting are achieving higher engagement and trust levels. Those companies make sure that managers are held accountable for using the performance management software. It makes their jobs easier. When managers can't see their team members' progress toward their goals, they tend to feel they have to micromanage. The software makes it unnecessary for managers to have to constantly collect information about what their direct reports are doing and what their competing goals might be."*
"I would encourage job seekers to ask managers how much the organization is helping them in doing their job of managing employee performance. We also see that there is a lot of empathy fatigue on the part of managers. Many managers are asking 'who's taking care of me?' I'd also suggest asking HR at your next employer about what tools, such as software, the managers have for managing performance."

Lynne Nelleman: *"Feedback may not come to you in an organized way. Google the Amazon.com list of Jack Welch's top 55 'good reads'--his own books and those of other senior executives. Jack was one of America's top CEOs. He was trained as a chemical engineer. While holding the position of Chairman and CEO of General Electric, he required his top 300 executives to get a 'mentor' who was at least 10 years younger and more proficient in technology. At GE it was 'modeled' in an organized way; you won't find that very often, but you can ask for feedback in as few as six months on the job. I've always liked what he wrote in one of his books: 'Control your own destiny or someone else will.' Another book I recommend is Adapt: Why Success Always Starts with Failure, by Tim Harford."*

Steve Puente: *"I taught managers how to do performance coaching for 15 years, but in my experience, most managers are not good coaches and won't initiate giving coaching and feedback. So, if you want feedback, and everyone does, you need to take charge and ask for it. The main thing is to have goals and focus on doing a great job."*

Applying Insights from our Panelists: Good Questions

Benefit from the advice from our panelists to assess if employers are committed to coaching and feedback. Key questions for your consideration:

- Does the prospective employer hold managers to account for the development of their associates? If so, how?
- Does the company address performance issues quickly and candidly, with an eye to helping employees address performance gaps?
- Does the employer have ongoing methods of providing and receiving feedback, such as surveys or "360 feedback" tools?

- Are there ways to receive feedback from "customers" you serve, either internal or external?
- Is their performance review process only annual, or is it a more ongoing process where you would receive feedback and coaching more frequently?
- What development programs are available, such as leadership training or mentoring?
- What do recruiters who are involved in hiring tell you about the coaching and feedback resources?
- How are remote employees provided coaching and feedback in a way that they're being remote doesn't penalize them?
- How about "reverse mentoring" -- is that available for older employees who might need coaching and feedback?

What Smart Employers Are Doing to Enhance Coaching & Feedback:

- Providing intensive feedback and coaching to new hires
- Creating cultures of continuous feedback
- Training all managers in performance coaching
- Holding managers accountable for coaching and giving feedback
- Making the performance management process less controlling and more of a partnership
- Not hesitating to terminate nonperformers when best efforts to coach don't pay off

Employers That Excel at Coaching and Feedback:

Brasfield and Gorrie (General Contracting), #1 Best Place to Work in Atlanta, 2021)

The company offers access to a "personal development manager" with whom they can speak confidentially on most any topic. One employee said she likes working at the company because "no one micromanages you. But you are expected to get your job done and do the right thing."

Winchester Hospital won Best Place to Work in Boston for six years in a row partly because it invested in a leadership program for managers. Managers attended 40 hours of leadership training that included intensive self-assessment, how to give and receive feedback, and how to have difficult conversations with colleagues and direct reports. Managers who were fearful of conflict and hesitant about confronting employees about non-performance were invited to rehearse the conversation with an HR coach.

Peachtree Planning, a financial advisory firm, has been recognized as a Best Places to Work in Birmingham, AL. The firm sets a standard: consistent feedback and set reviews with staff, 90-day team planning meetings and continually looking for opportunities to enhance the firm, culture, and morale. Of particular importance for the firm's next generation of advisors is coaching, development, and focusing on exposure and reach to meet with younger candidates.

Here are some additional questions for you to consider, based on the best practices of successful employers:

- If you are hired, can you get a "personal development" resource, who can help you with your growth and developments?
- How well are managers trained to provide coaching and development?
- If applicable to you, are there coaching and development resources for younger employees who are starting their careers?

Lens #6:

Will I Learn, Grow, and Advance?

Malcolm: A Merger Changes the Rules of Engagement

Malcolm loved his employer. He had been promoted a couple of times to a director-level and believed he had opportunities to continue his career growth. His next step would require him to take a lateral move to gain additional experience in finance and operations. But five years into his tenure the company merged with another company that had a different view of middle management. Rather than promoting from within, the new leadership team preferred to look outside the company to provide what they considered to be "fresh thinking." Malcolm concluded: "After the merger I knew my chances of continuing my career growth were more limited. As much as I loved the company and my team, I knew I had to move on. As soon as my 401(k) was fully vested, I was on my way."

This story illustrates the hard reality that sometimes the employer you join can become a very different employer during your time there, in this case through a merger with another company that apparently did not value hiring from within.

Research studies consistently reveal that limited career opportunity is a major driver of career dissatisfaction. Most managers lack competency in developing their direct reports and many workers believe that the only available path to career advancement is by leaving their current employer.

Our analysis of employee exit survey comments revealed several clear and consistent themes:

Unclear Career Path:

"There was no clear direction for those who didn't know what they wanted to do. Clearly defined career paths were not available."

"It would be great to have better insight into what the future for me looks like here. What does management have in mind in terms of where the team should be and what my future role in it can be."

"My manager never even asked me about my career goals."

Limited or Too Slow Career Advancement:

"There is not much opportunity to move up. You get entrenched in a position and you're stuck there."

"Promotions and advancement outside a department within the company are not easy to accomplish."

"I have been pressured to stay and been promised things that I have been working for, but they are never fulfilled, and I am looking for a different job."

Not Hiring from Within

"I have seen four supervisors hired within one year--all of them from other companies. Promote from within first!"

"The company does poorly regarding promoting from within. We had internal candidates who could have stepped in and done the job quite nicely."

Lack of Opportunity to Learn or Get Training:

"My leader didn't understand my job or their job which made training non-existent."

"The training classes were great, but my manager nixed my requests to attend because we were always too busy."

"The main reason I left is because I found an alternative opportunity with proven leadership and that will be a positive challenge. However, if I were 100% satisfied in my current position, I would not have been open to hearing about other opportunities. Given the role and current

leadership, I did not feel in the position I was learning or getting the credit for the work that I did do."

Unfairness or Favoritism in Promotion Decisions

"There's a lack of consistency in policy and standards when it comes to applying for new roles."

"I was being held back by my manager who didn't want to lose me, so he wouldn't recommend me for another position I really wanted."

"The director was appointed without the position being posted. Several other candidates had more integrity, management experience, and education than the director who was selected. It sickened the team."

AND YET...Some Employers Are Getting It Right

Survey comments of employees who were happy in their workplaces mirrored the same themes, but in a positive direction:

"Each day you learn something new, and there are new challenges day after day."

"Management asks about our interests and learning goals and keeps us up to date on the most in-demand areas of knowledge in the future and prospects for the company's growth."

"I love the many different tasks I am assigned to do--the variety of tasks, the challenge of trying to perfect my abilities."

"I have been developed as more than just a worker and leader, but also a human. My life would be way less positive without this job."

"This organization has helped me with my communication skills tremendously and the customer service training is through the roof."

What the Research Reveals:

Having opportunities to grow and advance makes a big difference in how we feel about our work. According to research conducted by BI WORLDWIDE, there is a strong correlation between happiness on the job and whether you see a future at your employer:

- Employees who felt they received the right training were twice as likely to feel inspired, but employees who felt they received training that was not useful were twice as likely to be uninspired by their work experience.
- Employees who know their next career step are more committed to their company than those who do not. It is important for everyone, but particularly important if you are 45 years old or younger.
- One of the top predictors of commitment and performance is the ability for an employee to see their future for themselves.

Did the "Great Resignation" of 2020-2022 Lead You **To Reassess Your Career Options?**

Given extra time to think, many have been feeling an even stronger need to see specific opportunities for growth and development. The studies vary on the overall percentage of us who feel this way, but it's a growing trend.

The need for clarity in this Lens has, according to our research, always been important, but heightened awareness of where we may have opportunities for continued growth and development is yet another consequence of what we've experienced together from the pandemic.

If you're one of those who feels this lens is important, insist on clarity with prospective employers.

Three Fundamental Needs

In this chapter we focus our lens on three basic needs we all have:

1. The need to stay happily challenged and engaged by activities of the job itself
2. The need to keep learning and acquire new skills and knowledge
3. The need for opportunities to advance on our career paths

Staying Happily Challenged

There is a more-or-less predictable cycle that new employees go through. The new job can be overwhelming at first until you begin to get a handle on the new environment and the new and different tasks and problems you face. Within a few months, most new hires enter a period of relatively smooth sailing, depending, of course, on the degree of disruption in the industry, the stability of the organization and its leaders, and often its speed of growth. Some people become bored when they have begun to master the job tasks or have achieved a significant goal and if they do not find a new challenge to re-engage them, they become indifferent, less effective, and sorely in need of a new challenge.

Some of us get bored more quickly and are prone to look for new challenges more frequently than others. Others, by contrast, never seem to get bored or grow tired of taking on the same kind of challenge day after day using the talents they most enjoy. A counselor, for example, may want to remain in the same counseling job for years as long as he or she continues to see each client as a new and inviting challenge.

One of the benefits of analyzing your seven most satisfying accomplishments in Lens #1 is that you probably detected a pattern in the type of satisfactions you felt after each of those achievements. Take another look back at your Achievement Story pages and your answers to the question: "What was the Outcome...and Why was it Satisfying?" to remind yourself of the satisfactions you felt and the kind of challenge you might be seeking again. If you have consistently sought that satisfaction in the outcomes of your accomplishments, you will most likely seek it again and find it fulfilling.

If your next job does not present you with the opportunity to take on the kinds of challenges and satisfactions you are naturally inclined to seek, you will likely be frustrated and become disengaged.

For a more thorough and systematic approach to identifying the motivations that drive the kind of challenges you should be seeking, we recommend you take the in-depth assessment available for a fee at MotivationCode.com.

Your Need for Learning and Developing New Skills

Self-driving cars and passenger drones...oh my! With the pace of technological and societal change accelerating each year, staying abreast of the latest developments and new technologies in your field has never been more important.

Here are just a few of the knowledge areas that are projected to be most in demand in the coming years:

Cloud computing	Artificial intelligence	Cybersecurity
Data mining	Sales leadership	Language translation
Mobile app development	Audio/Video production	UXdesign
SEO/SEM marketing	Blockchain	Industrial design
Digital journalism	Animation	**Supply chain management**
Healthcare administration	**HR management**	Scientific computing
Natural language processing	Social media marketing	Game development
Customer service systems	Computer graphics	Accounting
Corporate communications	Project management	Strategic partnerships

...and many more too numerous to list and growing by the day, including sub-knowledges within each of the above.

Still, there are even greater concerns than which knowledge areas are most marketable and in demand, such as:

- What knowledge areas reflect your genuine and ongoing interests and enthusiasms?
- Will your next job call on you to use the areas of expertise you listed in Lens #1?
- Will you be able to acquire, add to, or refine the knowledge areas that you listed there as well?

Dave's Request for Training Doesn't End Well

Dave felt stuck in an advertising account executive job with a "nightmare boss" and desperately wanted to "get out from under". A client's husband had started a company with a creative product that appeared to have found a unique niche in the marketplace. Dave was intrigued. After two interviews the firm's owner/founder offered him the job. He was somewhat reluctant to accept it. After having dinner with the owner, Dave remembered "there was like a tinkling bell in the back of my brain sounding a little alarm that something wasn't quite right." I couldn't help noticing there was something dark about his personality and his world view. I should have paid more attention to that little bell."

Dave decided to take the job anyway. He negotiated an attractive salary and bonus, plus the commute was short. The job required Dave to get up to speed on some very complicated technology. When he asked the owner for some training, he was told, "I'm no trainer...you can figure it out." From that point on, the two men could hardly stand to be in the same room with each other. "It got really ugly," Dave recalled.

"I was failing to meet his expectations and he was failing to meet mine. There were many sleepless nights. I was questioning my abilities, but I couldn't bring myself to quit. I kept hearing my late mother's voice saying, 'You can make it...just stick it out...you can prevail at anything.'" After a few months he finally fired me. I should have talked to a couple of his clients or to other employees before taking the job. And I should have at least asked about how much training I would get. But I was too anxious to leave the previous job. It's always better to move toward a new job than away from one."

One study found that 62 percent of employees prioritize "the opportunity to rapidly develop skills" as an important expectation, yet only 33 percent said their companies were providing it." Leaders and managers at many employers still balk at providing training for fear that it will turn out to be a bad investment because the employees they train will just leave and take their skills elsewhere. The research on the impact of training on employee retention refutes this fear-- employees today tend to stay with employers who continually help them build their skills...and their resumes for the day they may eventually move on. In response to the common refrain "What if we train 'em and they leave?", we say, "What if you don't train 'em and they stay?"

Companies in *Fortune* magazine's annual listing of 100 Best Places to Work in America typically average 40 hours of training (five full days' worth) per employee per year.

If training and skills development is as important to you as it is to most people, here are a few questions you need to ask of a prospective employer (or future colleagues) during the interview process:

- Can you tell me about your onboarding and initial training process?
- Would you describe the kind of training you provide in a typical year?

- Are managers expected to work with employees to develop a yearly individual development plan (IDP)?
- How much training is self-paced online vs. in-person?
- Do you have a collaborative intranet capability such as real-time bulletin boards that allow employees to share knowledge?
- Do you reimburse for work-related college courses completed onsite or through eLearning?
- Do you pay for employees to attend industry conferences?

Regardless of what kind of resources and support for training the employer offers, keep in mind that you are responsible for asking the right questions and taking the initiative to pursue your own learning and development.

Career Advancement Means Different Things for Different People

The traditional idea of moving up the corporate ladder and thereby gaining increased power, status, responsibility, perks, and pay remains the goal of millions.

But not everyone is suited or motivated to make the climb. Some would rather advance by deepening their expertise or becoming known as an expert or authority in their field. These folks tend to be more focused on deepening their knowledge via further training or by taking on projects that require and deepen their expertise. They may be happy staying in the same job for years as long as they stay challenged and receive fair and competitive increases in pay.

Others seek breadth instead of depth. They define advancement as moving into experiences that build on previous positions and broaden their portfolio of skills and talents. They may move to a very different type of job after a few years if they can grow and be creative and are often open to rotational and cross-functional assignments.

There are also some who seek to change jobs often for the variety, independence, and exposure to new experiences, even if they are unrelated to their previous experiences. They may move from one temporary job to the next or, as consultants, they may move from one client project to another.

So, what does career advancement mean to you?

Look back at your responses to the *"Rewards for Your Efforts"* checklist in Lens #1. If you checked the items "Be in charge," or "Advance/Be promoted", for example, you may be more interested in the career ladder definition of career advancement. (This is not to say that those with different motivations should not pursue or would not succeed in a supervisory or management position.)

To illustrate further, if you checked "Master a craft/process" or "Learn/Gain expertise", you may be more suited to pursuing a technical career path with an engineering, scientific, university, or research-based organization. (Again, not having one of these motivations would not necessarily preclude you from pursuing and succeeding in a technical career path). If a technical career path is your goal, you will want to find out whether your next employer has instituted a series of steps whereby you can gain increasing levels of pay and recognition that are appropriate to your contributions.

If you are more interested in pursuing a variety of experiences and taking on new and different challenges or areas of knowledge, then you will want to know whether your next employer makes it easier to move horizontally within the organization. It used to be the case that a lateral move within organizations was seen as questionable or as a demotion. Now, to retain talent most employers allow employees to move laterally, or even down, if the move presents an opportunity to learn new skills or gain experience that will help prepare them for future promotions. Some employers even refer to these moves as "lateral promotions."

Again, the insights you will gain from investing in the previously recommended MotivationCode.com assessment will be especially valuable in determining what "career advancement" means to you.

Questions to Ask

Whatever career advancement means to you, here are questions that are reasonable to ask your next employer:

- What are the options for career growth from this position?
- Is there a typical career path or ladder?
- (To the interviewer) What was your path into your current position?
- How have others progressed from this position within the organization?
- Is there a requirement that employees stay in their jobs for a set period before moving on to a different job?
- Does the organization allow, and even encourage, lateral moves?
- Can you tell me about someone who successfully moved laterally?
- Does the organization focus more on hiring from within or from outside?
- Do managers typically allow employees to move on to other positions?
- Are all jobs posted internally before being advertised externally?
- Is there a policy requiring that internal candidates be interviewed before outside candidates?
- Does the organization keep employees well informed about its strategy and prospects for future growth and success?
- Does the organization provide tuition reimbursement or pay for external training that enhances effectiveness in the job or help prepare for future positions?
- Do you have a mentoring program or process?

What You Can Do to Create Your Own Growth and Advancement Opportunities

All the above questions are focused on what the employer does to encourage the career growth of its employees. But ultimately, it is up to you to take charge of your own career growth and initiate moves that advance your career. Here are some ways you can be the prime mover in your next job:

- Master the job you have now, first and foremost. Remember that fortune favors those who do a brilliant job today.
- If you find yourself in the wrong job, change to the right one. Love what you do, which means figuring out who you are in terms of talents, interests, values, and motivations (see Lens #1).
- Know how money flows through the organization, what factors cause profit and loss, and what part of that you can influence or control.
- When no promotional options seem open, seek lateral or cross-functional assignments, or create a job that meets unmet company needs and makes use of your talents (see chart below)
- Seek continual learning by both formal and informal means.
- Familiarize yourself with career paths of those in positions to which you aspire, gain their advice, get realistic previews of their jobs, and ask them to be a mentor to you.
- If a position you want is not currently available, seek mini assignments that will help prepare you and will give you the opportunity to try out "pieces" of the desired job.
- Exhaust all options for enriching your current job by seeking new challenges and more satisfying tasks and conditions in your current job before applying for other positions.
- Communicate your aspirations, talents, ideas, and plans to your manager so that he or she can provide appropriate feedback, coaching, or sponsorship.
- Re-energize your career by acting like an entrepreneur, starting a new service, more efficient process, line of business, or revenue stream for the company.
- Before deciding to leave your next employer, communicate to your manager or to a trusted mentor the source of any career frustration you may have and ask for ideas and assistance.

"FIND-A-NEED-AND-FILL-IT" OPTION FINDER GRID*

There are many ways to move, grow, and advance without leaving your current employer. This grid will help you focus on areas in the organization where changing circumstances may have created a need for your exact set of skills. Remember: "A job is a talent that meets a need."

	Your Work Unit	Another Work Unit	Another Dept.	Organization-wide
An unrecognized opportunity				
An "impossible" situation				

A new or emerging problem				
A roadblock, bottleneck, chronic shortage, weakness or limitation				
A challenge in the interface between different groups				
A missing piece in a pattern or sequence				
An underutilized resource				
An unexpected failure or success				
A non-existent, but needed service				

* Adapted from William Bridges, "Job Shift" Seminar Guide, William Bridges & Associates, 1996.

Our Panel of Experts Share Their Insights on Challenge, Growth, and Learning:

Renny Arensberg: *"We initiated inexpensive ways to engage our case managers, such as book club discussion groups and sharing helpful articles on stress management and other relevant topics."*

Ed Baldwin: *"If career advancement is important to you, ask the boss if there is someone who was moved laterally into a more responsible growth position, like an engineer moving into a training team. This can show to what extent the organization allows alternative paths for growth."*

Sherry Benjamins: *"I challenge learners to sponsor themselves and link up with those who can be their sponsors. One of them said, 'I can't introduce myself to the CEO, can I?' 'Why not?' was my response. I recommend building a network inside the company. Ambitious young people want to be a part of the strategic planning of the company, so we have them map out who the strategic influencers are in the organization and seek out their advice. Job candidates and new hires both should ask the question, 'How does someone succeed and thrive in this company today?' or 'What does a superstar look like in this culture?' and 'What happens when people fall short of expectations?'"*

Rick Beyer: *"Find out if the employer promotes from within. Do they conduct evaluations to identify high potential employees? How do they help people grow? What kind of training programs do they have? Are internal job opportunities posted for all to see? Do they have succession plans? Is their philosophy of employee development thoughtful and intentional or haphazard and sink-or-swim? For example, the U.S. military has a reputation for having highly intentional training, development, and succession planning regimens that may exceed even those of many civilian organizations. The key is to ask about whether those processes exist and to evaluate them. Also find out if they have a job posting program--is it professionally managed or perfunctory?"*

"First and foremost--perform well! Go deep in your knowledge, like doctors, lawyers, and scientists. Be willing to make a lateral move to become more diversified in your skill sets. Acquire more skills by getting involved civically. Speak up--articulate your objectives. Convey your aspirations. Seek mentoring, ask for career coaching. Raise your hand. Don't get prematurely discouraged before you've exhausted the potential opportunities. I'm proud to say I saw and pursued a growth opportunity for myself by identifying the need for a previous employer to become more strategic with HR."

Gary Bolles: *"Before you know how you want to grow, you need to know what success will look like for you—what's your Northern Star or Southern Cross. Many people are not self-driven enough to know that, so they look for external market signals of job/career requirements and success. You should look for organizations where everybody knows who the Chief Learning Officer is or whoever's in charge of creating a culture where continuous learning is valued. Novartis sponsors a "Curiosity Month" focused on dramatically proving their commitment. Look for organizations that have reduced the friction between work roles and view talent as an enterprise resource, not as talent owned by the individual's manager.*

"Many companies have poured glue on their job classifications, so they are silos and lateral career moves are nearly impossible. Fluid organizations can assemble teams based on skills needed, and the nature of the problem or project without having to overcome rigid structures that create friction. Find out whether your prospective employer views talent as a wholly owned resource and whether they make the skills on the team available to others."

Dennis Boyer: *"In interviews be careful not to ask too many questions about your prospects for promotions. You may come across as not sufficiently interested in the current role and more interested in future roles. If you're not a finalist candidate, you could come across as a potential problem employee. However, you could say 'One of the job attractions is how you can help me grow...Can you share with me what that might look like?' After getting hired, take responsibility for tracking your accomplishments and bring them up in the review process. Helping your boss to track and document your performance is in your own best interest."*

Bill Ellermeyer: "*A lot depends on the growth and success of the company. In a mature company, career stability--just staying in the job, may be more realistic than advancing to the next level. In a fast-growth company, rapid advancement is more likely to happen. Always ask how the company is performing. Some are in trouble. Many start-ups are under-funded and don't have enough runway to sustain success. I know a VP of Finance who was shocked after taking the job to find out that the company wasn't profitable."*

Mark Ernst: *"Ask the interviewer how frequently people get promoted. Where did the leadership team come from? Were they brought in from the outside or did they rise within the organization? Ask about their training philosophy and programs. Do they see employees as assets to be taken care of and invested in or just overhead expenses to be relentlessly managed? Is their training program interactive and robust or just an online library you must access on your own time? Do they allow people to move horizontally when vertical movement is blocked? In other words, do they embrace depth and breadth as ways to grow, not just climbing the career ladder?"*

Andrea Hendricks: *"Job seekers need to figure out what is important to them. Where do they want to go with their careers? Managers should be trained to help their employees think about their career options and help them achieve their personal goals. Developing people is good for business."*

Bill Holland: "*Talk to others who work there about their path, progress, and how they found and pursued opportunities. You can't read about it in any personnel manual. I always emphasize the importance of establishing good relationships with your colleagues in advancing your career in the organization. A college degree doesn't guarantee you anything but perhaps an actual interview. You need to understand the informal rules and relationship networks."*

Lynne Nelleman: *"Stagnation in your job is a killer. It kills initiative, morale, and eventually you'll either start disengaging or leave the company. Recent reports about Covid-19's impact on industry have changed that...in your favor. Even the President has told companies to raise their pay scales! Employment was once a 'sellers' market with companies setting the rules but now it's what is called a "buyers" market with many potential employees essentially saying, 'no way*

I'm gonna work for you.' The tables are turning so once you're in the door, ask for feedback. Not only from your supervisor but also from someone in human resources, specifically requesting what skills are needed for you to progress to the next level."

Steve Puente: *"Understand that you are probably being interviewed not just for the job you are taking, but for the job after that. So, ask about long-range opportunities. Is the function or department you're joining growing or not? Also ask about the employer's strategic plan for profitable growth. Ask what training is offered but be prepared to get your own training if the company doesn't provide what you're looking for."*

Gordon Smith: *"Before taking the job, ask the boss and other team members, 'What kinds of people succeed and fail here?' After you're hired, keep asking internal customers. Take ownership of your own professional development. Don't rely on the company to initiate your career planning. Most employers are not as good at onboarding as they used to be. So, expect to hit the ground running and be responsible for introducing yourself to the team. Learn quickly how your job fits with the jobs of other team members and beyond."*

"Be willing to make a lateral move if it helps you to develop new skill sets. Knowing when you're getting stale and are ready for a new challenge is key. If you feel your boss is blocking your next move, your options are to either leave, or go to his boss or to HR for advice. There's a book I would recommend for reading the political environment as well--it's called Survival of the Savvy."

Applying Insights from our Experts:

If ongoing learning and development are important to you in your next role, consider these questions based on the advice of our experts:

Can you be confident the prospective employer has a genuine commitment to the learning and growth of employees?

- Can they tell you what percent of employees are promoted internally, versus hiring from the outside?
- Can they share with you how they support the growth and development toward a high-performing culture?
- Are there multiple ways for an employee to grow, which would include promotions but could be lateral moves or growth in the current role?
- Are managers trained to have ongoing career conversations with employees?

Employers That Promote Employee Growth and Learning:

Schneider Electric, worldwide energy management and automation company, has created an AI-driven platform, dubbed Open Talent Market, that matches internal talent with projects, jobs, or mentors across the organization to give employees more choices in determining their development and career paths, and to give multiple business functions additional access to talent. A second initiative is an innovation challenge, titled Dare to Disrupt, where employees can form their own teams and pitch business ideas. Successful teams can receive support from the company's internal incubation team to start their own external businesses or have the option to develop the idea internally. On the employees' end, it's a further opportunity to pursue career development; on the business end, it works to build a culture of innovation.

West Monroe Partners, #1 Best Place to Work in Los Angeles, 2020 (Tech Consulting)

"There is a genuine desire from the company to put people on projects they care about, give people stretch assignments, and develop the next generation of leaders. The company leadership's actions during COVID-19 demonstrated that they care about employees and the business. Decisions and communications were swift, clear, and frequent. The company rallied behind its co-workers experiencing tough life events, providing both professional flexibility and moral support to help them through."

Ameriprise, #4 Best Place to Work in Minneapolis-St, Paul, 2020 (Financial Services)

"Offers employees a full suite of professional development opportunities, including online courses, workshops, mentoring, networking, and peer-to-peer programs that position employees for growth and advancement. In 2019, employees and advisers participated in more than 2,500 training courses. Employees participate in more than a dozen business resource networks to promote a diverse and inclusive culture and provide opportunities for professional development, relationship building, cultural awareness and community service. These networks engage over 5,000 participants annually."

Airship, a Best Places to Work winner in Birmingham, AL has a specific plan and associated investment for employee growth and development: "We believe ongoing learning is critical for crew growth. We have a budget allocated for each employee for training, conferences, or books. We have dedicated 10% of our time each week for our crew to devote to learning, experimenting, and developing new skills."

Applying Insights from Successful Employers

There are employers who are truly committed to your growth and development. Here's what to consider based on the best places to work employers:

- Are "stretch assignments" common with this employer as a way of helping employees learn and grow?
- How did company leadership act in challenging times when it came to learning and development? In the pandemic, for example, was there still a commitment to this lens?
- Are there various ways for employees to learn based on their interests and needs, such as in-person and online training?
- What examples can a prospective employer share about "peer-to-peer" learning opportunities that are available?
- What resource networks are available for employees to join, and are these programs utilized widely?
- Does the company have a budget for the growth and development of each employee? If so, how much is this budget?

Lens #7:

Will I Be Valued, Recognized, and Respected?

"We are all motivated by a keen desire for praise."

—Cicero

CAN WE FIND A PLACE WHERE WE CAN HAVE THE "BEST AUDIENCE EVER"?

A group of high potential leaders were at a corporate meeting, and that evening there was a group dinner. For the entertainment there was a singer who was from a different generation and the group was initially not terribly excited.

But one of the leaders said: "Hey, let's be the best audience ever for this singer."

The group got excited about the idea and decided to be "the best audience ever" for the singer that night.

An engaged and attentive audience brought out the best in the singer, and the group ended up having a magical evening.

Our research clearly shows that when employees feel like they are recognized and rewarded in a way that is of value to them they will be more likely to stay and work hard for their employers.

We're at our best when we feel the appreciation of the audience.

Let's explore how you can find a workplace that celebrates you, that recognizes and rewards you for your contributions.

NEITHER SEEN NOR HEARD

Over the years we have heard many employees express real concerns about not being valued at work.

- **Not feeling heard:** *"I would like to see management begin to ask the employees what they want and stop assuming they know what we want or need. They are so off-base."*

- **A lack of appreciation**: *"For the most part I feel very underappreciated and underpaid. The management team here does not recognize employees enough. The Director will not even speak to us at times; she just acts like we are not there."*

- **No recognition for contributions:** *"My supervisor never acknowledges my hard work or my quality work. I ALWAYS give 110%, and my supervisor never offers praise, thanks, or even gratitude. My supervisor often passes off my ideas and my work as her own."*

- **Some employees are valued, but others aren't:** *"The company has a wonderful bonus incentive program for upper management, and a very nice commission program for sales, marketing, PRS, etc. There is absolutely no incentive plan for corporate employees (who are not executive management)."*

- **Compensation doesn't align with achievement**: *"There is no incentive for better performance since the best workers get the same raises as the laziest workers."*

- **Criticism but not compliments:** *"There is no hesitation to let us know what we're doing wrong, but not kudos for a job well done."*

- **Out of sight, out of mind:** *"This office never seems to receive any recognition in any kind of corporate newsletters or bulletins. Many of us feel isolated and ignored."*

- **No respect, and perhaps worse:** *"Management is not treating us with respect. They do not listen to us. We often worry about retaliation."*

Here are some additional employee survey[1] comments from employees who are, sadly, not feeling valued at work:

- *"The entirety of this organization, leadership and employees included, does not appreciate my department or our tremendous workload."*
- *"Leadership does a terrible job of noticing, let alone recognizing, employees who go above and beyond their job descriptions."*
- *"There's no incentive anymore."*
- *"We work in a world where people need immediate gratification for their hard work – not just compensation, but actual recognition.*
- *"I think the employees here want more company-wide, sincere recognition."*
- *"Recognize that people are working hard. It doesn't feel like management cares about people's effort; they only care if the work gets done."*
- *"Would a "thank you" be so hard?"*
- *"We need access to conferences and educational/technological tools that will help us grow and be productive."*
- *"Please, please, please consider each employee as a human being, not just a warm body filling a position. Respect people by assigning responsibilities based on their strengths and create incentive programs to motivate."*
- *"Note to board: threatening termination is not the kind of attention that employees want."*
- *"The company should base employee recognition and advancement on the employee's ability to do the job. Not on favorites."*
- *"Quit treating employees like elementary kids! Employee appreciation was a joke this year. Kids' games, really? We are all adults; give us some real appreciation."*

WHEN YOU ARE VALUED-- WHY THIS LENS IS IMPORTANT

The academic research is also quite clear regarding the importance of this lens. We may enjoy many aspects of a job, but if we don't feel valued and recognized we are far less likely to feel engaged and inspired for the long haul. According to research from BI WORLDWIDE:

- If you are inspired at work you're twice as likely to be there 12 months later.
- Employees who felt the incentives the company offered were fair were eight times more likely to find work inspiring.
- There are certain types of rewards that are more inspiring than others. Awards such as travel, experiences and luxury items are far more inspiring than cash or gift cards.
- A bit of healthy competition can inspire you. Those who compete for individual, or team incentives are far more inspired at work. Ask about what kinds of contests the organization offers.
- Will a prospective employer help you set challenging, but obtainable, goals? Those who have that opportunity are far more inspired than those who don't.

- To fully inspire employees, it is important to tap into both intrinsic and extrinsic motivation. Extrinsic motivation predicts your commitment to an organization, while intrinsic motivation predicts how hard you'll work and how inspired you'll be to bring your best ideas to work.
- If an employer provides written recognition when an employee does well, employees are twice as likely to be inspired than if they don't.
- If you are in a sales role, how much you feel appreciated will make a difference to you. Sales representatives who report their leaders do a better job of recognizing them are far more likely to be engaged than those who don't feel that way.
- Employees who have gone from working in an office to remote work may suffer regarding their inspiration at work. If you are taking a job for which you are going to work remotely, determine how you can maintain your inspiration, and ask the prospective employer what they are doing to maintain the inspiration of remote workers.
- How fair you feel your pay is will be impacted not only by the compensation and benefits package but about how you feel about the culture of the organization. If you don't feel you have choices that are meaningful, don't see work-life balance that meets your needs, and don't see opportunities to lead you're less likely to believe your pay is fair. Another way of interpreting this insight—if the culture is not healthy and inspiring you cannot pay a person enough to work there!

A list of possible employer-sponsored benefits– what do you value?

- Healthcare (medical, dental, vision)
- Performance Bonuses
- Sign-on Bonuses
- Disability Insurance (long-term and short-term)
- Free meals
- Retirement (401(k) or 401(b) or pension)
- Sick/parental leave
- Vacation time/holidays
- Childcare (free or low cost)
- Stock options
- Tuition reimbursement (for self or children)
- Remote work option, flexibility
- Free access to online or offline fitness platforms
- Free access mental health platforms, counselors, and therapists
- Free and personalized healthcare during pregnancy
- Yearly health checkups and discounted medicines
- Health awareness information sessions
- Financial management information sessions
- Opportunities to give back to the community

How Employees Feel When They Are Valued at the Best Places to Work

Companies with a winning culture think differently about valuing their employees, and it is felt by employees. In our book, *Re-Engage,* we saw the stark difference between employers who had won "best places to work" competitions and also-rans when it comes to being valued. Our friends at Quantum Workplace [6] (which conducts the *Best Places to Work* surveys) continue to report this stark difference.

Below are comments Quantum has found in employee engagement surveys that tell us what kind of recognition makes employees feel valued.

- *It's nice that we survey. It shows that the company actually hears what we have to say; it gives each employee a voice."*
- *"I feel appreciated during our Employee-of-the-Month nominations."*
- *"I really like the silly awards given out at holiday parties, like 'Best Barista' or 'Most Energetic on Mondays.'"*
- *"Our manager works WITH us; she doesn't just tell us what to do but shows us how and jumps in when it gets busy."*
- *"This company goes above and beyond in support of work-related higher education."*
- *"Evaluations throughout the year show that the company cares about the work we do."*
- *"The employees here value small incentives, general kindness, and 'thank you's' for a job well done."*
- *"Our employer does so much for us to make us feel that we are very important to the office. I do not have the words to describe it—I'd just like to say thanks."*
- *"I am always acknowledged for extra time put in or extra effort. I feel appreciated and valued. I am always treated with respect."*
- *"Our company does not micromanage. They completely trust you to do a great job without constantly checking up on you."*

The "Great Resignation" May Have
Led You to Reassess How You Want to Be Valued

If you're working hard and nobody is noticing, is it time to reconsider your career?

It's demoralizing to go to work every day and know you're going to be ignored, unappreciated or ignored.

You can do better.

Don't settle for workplaces where you're not valued. Perhaps there was a time when you felt you needed to "hang in" with an employer because there weren't good opportunities for you, or you felt like "one in the hand is better than two in the bush", even if what you had in hand was an employer who didn't value you.

There are plenty of employers who will see your talents and experience and reward you accordingly. And find a place where what is important to you is being delivered, in full measure. Don't settle.

HOW DO YOU LIKE TO BE RECOGNIZED?

In *Re-Engage*, we suggested managers identify the unique ways each of their employees would prefer to be recognized. Below is a list of ways employers recognize the contributions of their employees—pick four or five that are particularly important to you:

__Simple Appreciation	__Salary Increase	__Public Praise
__More Responsibility	__More Autonomy	__Fun Activity
__More Visibility	__Time Off	__Serve on Task Force
__More Flexibility	__Favorite Work	__Promotion
__Inclusion in Meetings	__Trophy/Plaque	__Learning/Training

__Peer Recognition   __Special Privilege   __Taken to Lunch

__Face time with the Boss   __Praised to Higher Ups   __New Assignment

__Thoughtful Gestures   __Cash for Great New Ideas   __Customer Recognition

When we conduct management workshops where we use this exercise, it is frequently the most highly rated section of the course. Think about these and other ways you prefer to be recognized. Ask prospective employers whether the ways you find most important are possible. If you don't get a sense that at least one or two of your preferred ways are possible with a prospective employer, that may be a red flag.

CALEB'S STORY: When One Person's Reward is Another's Person's Punishment

His first job out of art school was designing wrapping paper and gift bags for a company that specialized in Christmas accessories. Caleb found quick success--two of his designs were accepted for production and mass distribution within his first three months on the job. As a "reward", he was selected to be personally and exclusively mentored by a senior designer who was generally acknowledged to be the best illustrator of Santa Clauses in the U.S. She was planning to retire and was looking for a worthy successor.

Caleb was honored by the attention and recognition of his talent, but unfortunately did not embrace the vision or ambition of carrying on her legacy as a premier Santa illustrator. He needed a variety of artistic challenges and could not bring himself to disappoint her by declining to be mentored. But after a few months of learning what she had to teach him; Caleb was ready to move on. He applied for and was hired as an illustrator at a local ad agency.

Our esteemed panelists feel strongly about the importance of this lens:

Renny Arensberg: *"KVC Healthcare certainly can't compete with Amazon when it comes to salaries, so we look for candidates who are motivated to help others and buy into our mission. We introduced regular employee pulse surveys, and we typically have a 90-plus participation rate. We make sure every employee's voice is heard."*

Ed Baldwin: *"Just know that there are companies on the great places to work list because they pay well, but they do it to make up for their toxic cultures."*

Rick Beyer: *"Look them up on Glassdoor.com to see what current and former employees are saying. During information interviews with former employees ask if they recognize service anniversaries. Do they recognize employees in their newsletters? Do they give spot bonuses for exceptional performance?"*

"Look for clues during the interview process. How are you treated during the interview? Are you taken to lunch? Ask all coworkers during interviews how the company recognizes their contributions and makes them feel valued. Ask if their workstation was set up and ready on their first day. Was the company meticulous about introducing them properly? Did they have a purposeful onboarding process? What is the state of the physical environment, office space, devices, and accoutrements? Do they have special luncheons to recognize top performers? At one of my previous employers the CEO took us to an expensive restaurant to thank us for how hard we had all been working to complete a special project and announced he was starting a wellness program for all employees."

Gary Bolles: *"Your team guide (manager) needs to know what drives and energizes you, so you need to articulate it. You may need to negotiate during the interview for a change in your work role that allows you to use a talent you love. Just realize that your power is greatest at the moment before you accept the job offer as written. The employer you join should continually be looking for ways to recognize and give bonuses—the more random the better. Everyone on the team should feel like they could get "struck by lightning" (in a good way) at any moment by being praised and appreciated. Also look for an organization that wants your ideas and listens to your input. Do they invite engagement and new ideas across the enterprise and value all contributors? Do they understand that you don't lose power by empowering your team members, you gain power?"*

Dennis Boyer: *"Employers conduct reference checks on you. Do reference checks on the employer. Find people on LinkedIn who worked there and ask whether they have a culture that values people. Once hired, document your own accomplishments so you can communicate your value without being aggressively self-promotional. Prove you are adding value.*

Mark Ernst: *"Do they listen to everyone's voice? Do managers try to hear from everyone during meetings? Will you have a say in decisions that affect you?'* Try to find out how your prospective employer values top performers: *How do they recognize those who go above and beyond? Do they praise employees who stay late or work weekends to complete a project? Is their praise genuine and specific or vague and insincere?"*

Andrea Hendricks: *"Being valued is exceptionally important. I encourage job seekers to gain insights into what a prospective employer is doing to show they value their workers. People thrive on recognition. It keeps the innovative spirit alive. Companies need a diverse and strong recognition process. This should include peer-to-peer recognition. It can be verbal and nonverbal. Recognition should also be tied to performance."*

"Regardless of your role, outstanding performance should be recognized, as with sales or leadership, or diversity champion awards. Companies should reward what is important. If employers want their talent to aspire, then recognize them for their success."

Bill Holland: *"Find out if your prospective employer conducts employee surveys, takes them seriously, and takes action to make it a better workplace. The answers you want to hear are "Yes, but we are not as good as we want to be" or "Yes, but not as good as we thought we were" and "We want to get better." Know how you want to be rewarded for your contributions. Some people say you must sacrifice higher pay for more time off, but maybe you can have both. Lately there has been a groundswell of people who want more free time and remote work, and they are getting it."*

Lynne Nelleman: *"Demonstrate that others value you. By others, I mean 'movers and shakers' in your community. Quickly become an active volunteer in 2-3 nonprofit organizations. Your superiors will take notice if officers and/or boards of directors are prominent individuals in your community."*

"Many corporate employees at senior levels must have their outside activities approved; so, act more like a senior person! Write a memo to HR alerting them to these outside activities with a description of each organization. Include the names of all directors of that nonprofit, hospital, school/college/university, business bureau, or chamber of commerce including the title of directors where they work in their paying jobs."

"Find out if your division or departmental heads have allocated budgets to support employees' community service. Even if they don't have funds to support you/your mission, you've made them aware of leaders in the community who DO value and recognize you. Another approach is to speak with your company's Foundation president, prevalent in large corporations. Find out how you can be supportive of the Foundation's activities. Even if you can't because of your junior level or economic constraints, you've demonstrated knowledge of organizations that matter to your company."

"Trust me: if you become a valued volunteer, you become more of a valued employee. You are building community goodwill and contacts for your company. THAT will be appreciated, and YOU will be appreciated. A glowing media report for the place where you volunteer becomes an implicit pat on the back for you."

Steve Puente: *"If you're not feeling valued and not being recognized, it may be that you just have a bad manager. If that is the case, and it often is, you may just have to wait until you get a new manager or change jobs internally. Or it may be that you need to look in the mirror...maybe you haven't yet done enough to deserve recognition."*

Gordon Smith: *"Feeling devalued may mean my values don't match. This doesn't mean that your values are wrong, and a prospective employer is right. It means they're different, and we should carefully consider the impact of that mismatch regarding what is important—what we value—in comparison to what that employer values."*

Mary Kay Ziniewicz: *"For me and for many folks looking for meaningful work, being compensated for full-time work that doesn't allow for balancing family goals is a price too high. Employers need to recognize and value moms. We want to make sure moms are cared for. This is advice we believe should be applied to job seekers who are thinking about work that fits our needs, including how we're compensated.*

Applying Insights from Our Experts: Good Questions

Our experts have again provided exceptional advice. Questions you should consider asking:

1. Does the organization celebrate successes that support the achievement of their mission? Does their mission "speak to you" in a way where you would be excited about receiving such recognition?
2. Do the pay and benefits give evidence of a culture that is caring, or are pay and benefits provided as a way of making up for an otherwise toxic culture?
3. As you are interacting with employees in the hiring process, can they share how they've been valued? Do they get excited sharing their successes and how they've been recognized?
4. What do former employees say? Were they valued, or did they leave because they didn't feel appreciated?
5. Do you get a sense that employee opinions are valued? Is employee feedback encouraged, even feedback that might not be viewed as positive? Can employees share in a way where they still feel "psychologically safe"?
6. Is recognition just for top performers, or are there ways for employees at all performance levels to be recognized when they contribute?
7. Are there formal processes for employees to regularly offer feedback and ideas, such as surveys or idea generation programs? If so, are they actively used and are employees who contribute provided appropriate recognition?
8. Are employee contributions to outside activities that benefit the community valued and appreciated? If so, how?

Employers That Are Known for Valuing, Recognizing, and Respecting Their Employees:

There are some employers who are doing an exceptional job of valuing their workers. Here are a few stories to give you a sense of what is possible:

- At the technology company **Motley Fool**, "the tech company decided that one day a year was simply not enough to recognize all the great things their employees do. That's why they made everyday Employee Recognition Day. They host fun events throughout the year and use a peer-to-peer recognition tool. The tool allows employees to give each other shoutouts that can later be converted into prizes. The program has been a success, with employees letting each other know about a job well done 35 times a day."[2]

- The online retailer **Zappos** "encourages employees to recognize each other's hard work through incentives. The program allows employees to give each other $50 for going above and beyond. This is just one of a variety of programs they offer. One is the Zollar Program, which allows employees to rack up points on a gift card that can be used to buy items like gym bags, water bottles, and desk fans. Producers Assistance has also run a similar gift card program in which many of its employees have participated.[3]

- Global hotel chain **Hilton** "provides managers an annual Recognition Calendar that features 365 no-cost and low-cost, easy-to-implement ideas to thank employees. The calendar includes reminders and tips for enterprise-wide, brand, and department recognition programs; appreciation best practices; important dates like International Housekeeping Week; and recognition quotes to share with employees. It also allows users to add employee service anniversaries and local events. Users can download a print-friendly PDF or import an Outlook-friendly file into their personal calendars."

Applying Insights from Engaging Employers: Good Questions

There are employers who do truly value employees and have programs in place that show their commitment to valuing employees. As you're looking at prospective employers, ask yourself these questions:

1. What formal programs does the employer have for recognizing and celebrating employee successes?
2. Is there a way for employees to provide "peer-to-peer" recognition, and is the program widely used?
3. Can all employees give a financial reward to another employee for going "above and beyond"?
4. Is there a formal calendar of events where there are company celebrations?
5. Does the organization have a way of sharing positive feedback with customers or outside stakeholders that can be directed toward individuals or teams who have successfully served outside parties?

Taking Action: Will You Be Truly Valued?

Below are a series of questions you can use to assess how a prospective employer values their associates. For the questions that are important to you…get feedback from multiple sources—current and past employees, suppliers, neighboring employers, etc.:

- Overall, would you say this is a company that values employees? Can you give me an example or two of why you say that.
- Do you have examples of when this employer acts in a way that might show that employees aren't valued and, if so, can you describe those times?
- Is this an employer who is known for fair and competitive pay?
- Is this an employer that has competitive benefits?
- In what way does this organization stand out as particularly special when it comes to compensation and benefits?
- What changes, if any, have you seen in the compensation and benefits of this organization since the pandemic began in the spring of 2020?
- Are there formal recognition programs at this company, and specifically for the kind of work for which I'm applying? Please give examples.
- What is the culture regarding informal recognition, such as appreciation from managers or team members?
- Does the organization have any special ways of recognizing employees? If so, what are they?
- Are you aware of any situations where people like me would have difficulty gaining employment with this organization?

Lens #8:

Will I Be Entering a Healthy Workplace Culture?

We noted this thread on social media:

"It's been 5 weeks since I left a toxic workplace. Since then, I've started working out for the first time in years. My wife says I'm a lot nicer. I see my daughter more. My therapist noticed a difference. Please, if your job is affecting your mental health, find a way out."

Another person on the thread continued:

"Well done! I had a job like that several years ago with an agency I worked for in London. The manager was toxic, and she destroyed the business from the inside... My partner noticed it was starting to have an impact on my personality and was like a brand new me after I left."

Another posted how much difference even one week in a new role can make a difference:

"Couldn't agree more. Thank you for sharing! I just recently left a toxic workplace and my new workplace honors employee mental health, and I already noticed the shift in my attitude towards myself and my husband and am just in week 2!"

"The slow drip of working in a high-stress long-hours industry had finally started to take its toll after 20 years. Once out and into a new industry it's hard to look back on and comprehend how or why I stuck it out for so long when alternatives were available."

And then there was this epic thread from Reddit:

"Twas the night before my resignation...

"I was brainwashed at an early age that loyalty and hard work would add countless "0's" to your paycheck. I remained optimistic after receiving year after year of 3% raises and working holidays. I missed my childrens' first steps, their school functions, and other life events so I could make my CEO more money.

"After the passing of my stepfather and my boss calling me during the funeral, asking me to troubleshoot an issue while my mom cried into my shoulder, enough was enough. I changed companies and made a personal pledge to put my family first and my career a distant third or fourth.

"Fast forward to present day.... I find myself the cornerstone of our department. Many of our clients' processes are automated through custom API developed by me. I have maintained a thorough documentation library on how to support the API, the reports, and all its dependencies. I have offered to train backup, so we are not single threaded. My manager told me 'No way, we would never do anything to lose you.' Up to now, life has been good.

"At the beginning of December, ABC Company was audited by the government and found to be out of compliance. They hired my company to regain their compliance by the end of the year or risk fines near $750,000. ABC Company dragged their feet getting us the information we needed to start the work.

"I save my vacation days so I can take the week between Christmas and New Year's off. I spend it with my kids to make up for the time I lost when I worked when they were younger. This time is very precious to me.

"Last week and this week I have been notifying the project manager and my manager about my time off. I let them know I would need ABC Company's information soon so I can start on it. I offered to work extra hours to ensure my piece would be finished prior to Christmas Eve.

"On Tuesday, my manager calls me and tells me ABC Company sent the data I requested over two weeks ago. He looked beaten because he knew what was about to happen. I told him who I should walk through the project with because I'm off after Christmas. My manager says, 'sorry, but I have to ask you to work. I declined your time next week.'

"I asked, 'What happens to my vacation time?' My boss says, 'I'm sorry. You know the rules. Use it or lose it. I fought for you, but HR wouldn't budge.

"I drafted my resignation letter after the call, set it to delay delivery on Monday at 8 am, and closed up shop.

"ABC Company will pay $700,000 because nobody knows how to program that system since there is no backup. Our other clients will be expecting their monthly, quarterly, and annual reports within the first week of January. No one knows how to do this. We had six projects in progress involving extensive API and reporting. Now those projects are dead in the water. Seven clients prepaid for API and automation upgrades in 2022 Q1. I don't know what will happen to those.

"Please remember. Family first. You never get that time back."

Update—Text messages responses from boss on Christmas Eve:

"Please call me as soon as you can…

"I received your email. I understand that you are upset, but resigning is not the best choice in this circumstance…

"I have been your friend for five years. I'm asking you as a friend, not a manager, to reconsider and call me. Let's talk about this…

"Hey, you made your point. You can have today off if you call me and let me know when we can expect you tomorrow. But you need to call me…

"This is ridiculous. Do you know what your actions are going to do to the company? To me? You made your point. Just call me and we will figure out your vacation. But we need to talk…"

End of thread.

And we find similar sentiments in surveys:

In employee surveys we conduct we have come across too many stories of employees who are struggling in cultures of sacrifice where stress and burnout are the norm and not the exception:

- *"I have been working in this industry for 15 years. I'm burnt out on working every weekend or holiday and missing out on time with my kids. I have also been in some type of management position and I'm ready to focus on my individual success without the pressure of management."*

- *"I just took my oldest daughter to college, and I realized I missed too much of her life being trapped in this job. In the past I was able to rationalize this because I made a significant amount of money and I felt worthwhile."*

- *"I am not paid anywhere near enough for the stress and anxiety I am experiencing."*

- *"Only favorites are preferred, and it doesn't matter how hard others work, I'm never appreciated."*

- *"The management team puts fear into its employees to work harder by saying they will fire us if we do not do the best job we could. I believe that if the management team starts to reward its employees for the good job they do and recognize the amount of stress they deal with daily then it will be a better work environment as well as higher pay than minimum wage. Then I will start recommending this job to my friends."*

- *"Staff are working 10-hour shifts to make up for the lack of workers and it is difficult to have a personal life with how much they expect their staff to work."*

- *"The leaders don't care about their employees when they are sick or something bad happens in their lives. They just demand work but have no sympathy for them."*

Thankfully, not all of us feel this way about their workplace. Here are folks who feel much better about this lens:

- *"I can work during the day while my 3 kids are at school, no nights, no weekends.*

- *"I can work shifts around my other job, and around family obligations. The manager works within my availability."*

- *"This job gives me the opportunity to pursue my future career goals without compromising any of my external responsibilities."*

The Themes that Emerge

Several themes emerge from these comments, which you should assess in your search:

- Having to work ***too many hours***,
- ***Personal life*** suffering because of work,
- A perception that ***pay-and-benefits don't compensate for undue stress***,
- Being demoralized because of ***favoritism***,
- Being the victim of ***fear-based tactics or intimidation***,
- Managers showing ***no empathy or compassion*** for associates.

Which of these factors would cloud your lens?

Burnout as a Brand:

There are some work cultures which celebrate taking employees to their physical and mental limits. One employer is well known for making "rich widows" because of how hard they drive their (mostly) male workforce.

A vice president of operations who proudly states, "I don't get stressed, I <u>give</u> stress."

Another boasts "we only work half days– seven to seven!"

And another has the reputation that managers will send emails during off hours and see how long it takes employees to respond.

Look closely at what you learn from job postings and networking conversations and then ask yourself…

… is burnout their brand?

Contributing Factors to Workplace Burnout and Undue Stress

In her book *"The Burnout Epidemic: The Rise and Fall of Chronic Stress and How We Can Fix It"*, Jennifer Moss summarizes her research into the six factors that can contribute to burnout and stress at work. Measure these factors with each of your prospective employers:

1. **Workload –** is a prospective employer asking too much or working at times which don't fit your lifestyle and goals?
2. **Perceived lack of control –** is the employer offering you a workplace where you'll have some measure of control over your work and an ability to impact outcomes?
3. **Lack of reward and recognition –** do you believe you'll be valued for your contributions in ways that are valuable to you as we discuss in Lens #7?
4. **Poor relationships –** do people generally get along at this workplace and do you get a sense they enjoy collaborating?
5. **Lack of fairness –** is there a sense that everyone has a fair chance and are treated with fairness?
6. **Values mismatch –** are the products and services a prospective employer offers in alignment with what is important to you?

Candace: Changing Life Circumstances Lead to Changed Priorities

Candice had a great job she loved at an advertising agency. For the first few years she didn't mind the 60+ hour work weeks, because the work was interesting, and she was paid well.

Then she and her husband started a family, and there was a greater desire for work-life balance. She found a company that also offered interesting work but didn't require the hours.

In her own words: "My new employer put right into the advertisement that they valued work-life balance. I knew a couple of people who worked there, and after a couple of calls to them they convinced me that they were serious about doing great work without me making sacrifices with my family. I've loved it ever since."

What the Research Says About This Lens

In our new jobs we will experience stress, perhaps even burnout on occasion. But prolonged stress and burnout can demoralize us, and even worse, can impact our health.

According to research from BI WORLDWIDE:

- When employees feel a sense of intrinsic and extrinsic motivation at work, they are less likely to feel burnout. It is extremely important we feel motivated for our work.

   From one report: *"The inability to find meaning in work better predicts burnout than does the number of hours worked. In a healthy workplace culture, people feel their job matters and see how it connects to larger organizational goals. They also believe their company is socially responsible and values its mission."*

- Employees who feel burnt out are much less likely to be working hard.
- Employees who are experiencing burnout aren't working more than those who aren't feeling burned out.
- What factors predict employees saying their workplace is healthy? If...
   - Their manager understands them,
   - Their ideas are taken seriously,
   - They're confident the good work they do will be recognized, and
   - Their job is challenging to them and pushes them to stretch their talents.

In other words, a culture that is inspiring is a healthy workplace.

- Employees who are easily able to get paid time off when needed are twice as likely to be working hard.

- Employees are more likely to feel isolated at work when they don't feel a strong sense of teamwork, so it's critical the culture fosters a sense of teamwork and collaboration.

Did "Great Resignation" Lead You to Reassess
Whether This Job Will Burn You Out or Energize and Inspire You?

Let's be fair-minded about this--even in the best jobs there are times when we're going to work extra hard to meet an important deadline or take care of a valued customer. We can put up with a temporary time when we must expend extraordinary effort.

But if prolonged, it takes a toll.

For many of us, the pandemic took even more of a toll, impacting people across the economy.

As one person on social media commented: "Before the pandemic, many managers got away with a narrow focus on performance at work. Now, I hope more are recognizing that they can't afford to ignore well-being in life. You don't get quality work when people are struggling with quality of life."

We agree.

In your reassessment, consider how important this lens is to your personal and professional goals.

Is Anyone Surprised that Work Culture Has a Significant Impact on Your Physical Health?

There is scientific proof: A study by Professor Brad Shuck at the University of Louisville, published in The International Journal of Environmental Research and Public Health, indicated that organizational culture plays a huge role explaining why some people are at elevated risk of getting sick and developing long-term chronic diseases.

Old vs. New Mindsets about Employee Well Being

In our book, **Re-Engage** we wrote about companies having different mindsets about how they would invest in the wellbeing of their employees. They tell a story of companies who are taking very different approaches to the well-being of their employees. Although the business climate and conditions such as the pandemic have emerged, these mindsets feel even more relevant. Look for evidence of these mindsets in your search:

Old Mindset	**New Mindset**
Some employers are just trying to "get by", offering only the bare minimum of resources…	… while others are making genuine efforts to meet the needs of their employees.
Some employers see their workforce only in the context of what happens during work hours…	… while others realize that employees have lives outside of work that must be understood and appreciated.
Some employers are making it the "problem of the employee" by directing all additional costs to the employee side of the balance sheet…	… while others work to collaborate in partnership with the employee.
Some employers blindly continue paying more health insurance claims related to diseases largely seen as driven by poor lifestyle…	…while others want to "fix the problem before it starts" by emphasizing prevention and well-care practices…
Some employers see benefits as an expense that drains resources from the bottom line…	… while others see benefits as a long-term investment that can reap generous returns by making employees more productive.
Some employers see benefits as a "one-size-fits-all" proposition, harking to the words of Henry Ford who told buyers they could have their car any color they want as long as it was black…	… while others look to tailor their offerings to meet the needs of various constituent groups of employees who may have different needs.

A Checklist for Evaluating Employers in Difficult Times

We also recommended a series of practices for "difficult times", which we present as a checklist for you to consider. Does a prospective employer:

1. ___Communicate the availability and value of *all* benefits?
2. ___Conduct surveys and/or focus groups to find out what new benefits are truly needed?
3. ___Hold meetings where employees can put their life-work responsibilities on the table and work out ways to give and take so that both personal and work commitments can be met?
4. ___Make employees more alert to signs that coworkers may be burning out over becoming over-stressed? We know of one company that asks employees to report situations where employees are in the "red zone"--putting in several consecutive weeks of 60+ hours or long periods without time off. The company has "interventions "with these employees, insists that they take time off, and finds ways to assure the employee's work gets done during their absence.
5. ___Educate employees about stress/time management, healthy diet, exercise, and lifestyle? Hold on-site health screenings, help subsidize health club memberships, etc.
6. ___If "takeaways" must happen, such as suspending the employer retirement match, clearly communicate the decision, the reasons behind it, and try to restore that benefit as soon as possible?
7. ___Encourage fun activities and employee get-togethers to build cohesion and relieve stress?

Not all employers may meet each of these standards, but if you have concerns about the answers to several of these questions it should give you pause as to whether that employer is committed to this lens.

Are You About to Enter the Twilight Zone?

In the very first episode of The Twilight Zone, which aired in 1959, a man (played brilliantly by Earl Holliman) who was apparently suffering from amnesia, found himself in a town where there were no other people. He occasionally felt the presence of others, but never made contact, was never able to communicate with others, to share his fears and concerns.

We know workplaces like that.

People can feel very lonely in certain workplaces, even those with people all around them.

In the case of the Twilight Zone episode, it turns out the whole thing was the delusion of an astronaut who was training to be alone in space. He had been in isolation for many days and was feeling the effects.

Loneliness can do that.

Some jobs, such as astronaut, may need to put up with being alone, but in most cases we can look for work cultures where there is a feeling of collaboration and community, where communication is open and folks feel connected.

Do your homework about each prospective employer. Do they value building community?

Don't end up in your version of The Twilight Zone.

Our Panel of Experts Share Their Views on Employee Well Being:

Andrea Hendricks: *"Stress is part of life. Each person needs to understand how to manage it, but the organization can minimize stress by offering benefits. You must ask yourself 'can I gain the confidence of my company where I can flex work to do my job and still meet my personal needs?' Can I flex my day or my week? That may be ideal for many, but difficult for others--not knowing my work schedule for more than two days ahead, for example."*

"But if you select an essential role with your employer, then you have a commitment that may make your ability to flex more difficult. If you select a role, you can't hold the company hostage. You need to see if that choice makes sense for you. You need to know the consequences of imbalance. Evaluate your own needs and your family's needs for balance and well-being. What are you willing to trade off? Check out the reputation of your future manager and employer."

Renny Arensberg: *"Our organization, KVC Health Systems, provides medical and behavioral healthcare, social services, and education to disadvantaged and displaced children. The work is stressful for the company's case managers who interact directly with fragmented families and abused, suffering children. Every case is urgent and stress levels are made worse by frequently having to work with parents who do not want to work with them. Many of the children have severe emotional issues and some are engaging in self-harm or considering suicide. "*

"As a result, first-year case manager employee turnover can be high. So, we leaned into taking care of our case managers with our heart and soul. We do regular pulse surveys to listen to their concerns and we take action to address concerns. We get a 92 percent response rate to these surveys. Our compassionate response during the pandemic has reduced turnover."

Ed Baldwin: *"Consider taking a pay cut and taking a 'life raise.' If the prospective employer says, 'we work hard and play hard,' ask 'How do you play hard?' How do they measure success? How do they manage work-from-home scenarios?"*

Rick Beyer: *"I don't think there is such a thing as work-life balance. But there is good stress and bad stress, and your mindset has a lot to do with which one you are feeling. The key is enjoying your work and purpose in life so your purpose fuels your energy and motivates you to work long hours. I haven't known anyone who was very successful who only worked 40 hours a week. Healthy food, exercise, flexible hours, remote or hybrid working options, and childcare all can help to support wellbeing and manage stress. The company where I used to work didn't charge for food in the cafeteria and made sure it was nutritious. Food choices were clearly marked to* *indicate the most nutritious selections and those that were less nutritious, but nevertheless tasty. Look for leaders who appreciate the flesh and blood behind the numbers."*

Gary Bolles: *"Many organizations push employees until they are a crisp, burnt hulk. But today's workers are valuing LIFE more than work, as evidenced by the enthusiastic reception of remote work starting in 2020. Look for an organization that knows you have a life outside work and is concerned about your overall well-being. Employers like CVS, for example, provide mindfulness training. Of course, you may be willing to work yourself half to death for three years to make enough money to pay off that college loan. It's up to you whether you make that trade-off and sacrifice your sleep and stress level for financial return.*

"I would advise job seekers to find out what the prospective employer's level of consciousness is about all the above. Do they expect you to respond to emails at night or on weekends? Do you get five weeks of vacation but are expected to only take one? Do they encourage social connections with other employees or not? Is the culture toxic or not? Are leaders inspiring or punishing? What about their mission-- does it inspire and energize you because you believe in it, or does it drain you because you don't? Do the leaders uplift you or make you cynical?"

Dennis Boyer: *"Work-Life balance is important for both employer and employee – both have a lot at stake here. Burn-out should be prevented by both parties. However, many companies don't display sufficient empathy about your stress level, personal well-being, or work-life balance. Be prepared to work long hours and do what it takes to get the job done. Try to think about what you are giving more than what you're getting. Sometimes burn-out occurs not just because of overwork but because the work increasingly lacks sufficient meaning. Many employees have found that volunteer work for nonprofit, charitable organizations in the community can enrich their lives beyond work. Sitting on a charitable board can add to your employer's positive reputation and enhance your career while serving as a growth-oriented professional experience and an enhancement to your community. For example, serving as a United Way chair for your company gives you much visibility, builds new relationships, and can lead to bigger career opportunities."*

Bill Ellermeyer: *"I had a client at a large tech company who reported that they take advantage and work people too hard. I also had a client who went to work for a Japanese company that expected evening and weekend work with very little time for family or leisure. He was making $400,000 a year, but he was stressed to the breaking point and his life was totally out of balance. Find people on LinkedIn who have worked at the company you are thinking of joining and asking about company culture, especially its approach to employee well-being."*

Mark Ernst: *"Will your boss send you emails at 10 pm and expect an immediate response? Or will the boss respect your personal and family time enough to wait until morning for you to respond? I loved having a CEO boss who insisted I take my vacation time. The best managers and employers do that because they know people need it. Ask about their holiday and vacation schedules. If you have to be employed there for seven years to earn a second week of vacation, that should give you pause. Do they trust you enough to expect you'll do your job without them having to hover over you? Do they allow you to work from home when possible and* *appropriate? During the interview, listen for phrases such as: 'work hard and play hard' or 'we all do what has to be done' and ask for examples of what that means."*

Bill Holland: "*I have yet to see an interview with higher ups that goes well when the candidate brings this up or emphasizes its importance. If work life balance is something a company values, they will likely mention it without you having to ask.*

Ann Maltese: "*Ask 'what processes do you have in place to support employee mental health? Do they have a holistic definition of wellbeing? Some companies instituted 'holiday quiet week' during the pandemic where there will be no client or customer meetings during the week before and after a major holiday, like July 4th or Memorial Day. During the quiet week, employees don't have to have their PTO approved and internal meetings are not scheduled. Employees know to preview this with their clients and don't schedule client meetings. This kind of practice addresses burnout at a structural level instead of just person by person. It also creates an equitable experience for both remote and onsite workers. Remote and hybrid workers often miss out on things those on-site workers hear about just because of daily personal contact. Some employees may miss some Zoom meetings as well and fall further out of the loop. Employers need to be sensitive about this."*

Lynne Nelleman: "*There's no way out of this conundrum. We can't live without stress. I have three favorite websites that help keep me from jumping off the cliff: www.verywellmind.com; www.positivepsychology.com and www.helpguide.org have excellent articles on stress management. Millennials are more focused on work-life balance than we Baby Boomers. I had my first-born son tell me I wasn't home enough, at the games enough, or cooking dinners enough. All of that is true. But would he have said it if I was his father, not his mother? Talk about bias in the workplace."*

"Do you or your employee's insurance plans meet some of your needs? X days of physical or mental therapy or medical leave? Educational support or opportunities? Salary scales? Vacation lengths? Availability of departmental rotations? The key to overcoming distress and dysfunction in the workplace is to identify someone you will be 'on your side.' One who can change policies and procedures. Laurie Santos, a professor of psychology at Yale, offers online classes on happiness. Author Celeste Headlee, a public radio host, has both a book and subsequent TED Talk on YouTube that was named #1 in Glassdoor's Must Watch TED Talks and #3 on CNBC's Top TED Talks of 2016. Her title? We Need to Talk: How to Have Conversations That Matter. You can be that someone, too."

Steve Puente: "*This is a tough one because very few companies really care about you having a balanced life. I spent years working 70-hour weeks, starting a job at 4:30 am and not getting home until 6:30 pm. So, I don't recommend asking about whether you can work from home or indicating that life/work balance is your top priority. Ask about their typical hours and vacation policies instead. Be prepared to work on being as efficient as possible in your job so you won't have to work longer hours. If stress becomes an issue, learn about personal stress management techniques such as using the Headspace app for meditation and relaxation."*

Gordon Smith: *"I was so stressed in one of my early jobs that I used to get sick to my stomach on Sunday nights. If you find yourself in a situation like that, and you hope the situation will change, it probably won't. There are things you can do to change your mentality and reduce self-imposed stress, but if the demands are unreasonable, you must scratch that employer off your list, or if you are already employed there, get out."*

Insights on Dealing with a Toxic Workplace from our Experts: Good Questions

Taking the advice of our experts can reduce the chances of you getting hired into a toxic workplace. Consider:

- What have you learned about how the leadership of this prospective employer dealt with stressful situations, such as the pandemic? Did they continue to support employees even in difficult times?
- Is there sufficient flexibility in the job requirements to meet your personal needs?
- If the job you are considering is considered "essential", are you comfortable with the requirements that may impact your work-life balance?
- Is there a part-time or work-from-home option with this role and, if so, will that impact how attractive the role is to you?
- Does the company expect you to "hit the ground running" or are they realistic and open about how long it may take for you to get up to speed?
- What can you learn about the culture of the company regarding being available at all hours? For example, are there any unwritten rules or protocol regarding responding to email or calls off hours?
- Was the interviewer able to describe how they helped employees deal with added stress and work/life complications during the pandemic?
- Will most of the work you will be doing bring you some sense of meaning or satisfaction beyond the pay and benefits offered?
- What do social media postings indicate about how current and former employees feel about work-life and burnout issues?
- Will the culture support taking time off from work to refresh?
- Does the company offer a compelling statement about their commitment to work-life and supporting the health of employees? Have they received any outside recognition for their efforts?
- Is there flexibility with work schedules that accommodate the needs of different employees?

Employers Who Are Promoting Employee Well-Being

RBC Wealth Management, *#1 Best Place to Work, Minneapolis-St. Paul, 2020**

"Provided a $300 stipend to allow employees who worked remotely because of the pandemic to purchase home office equipment to improve their working space. Other benefits included:

- *Emergency school closure leave for parents of children impacted by Covid-19-related school closures. The leave consisted of up to 20 PTO days for impacted employees.*

- *A special daily compensation program of $50 per day for employees working on site during the crisis, whether in our branches, operations centers or any location and role where working from home is not an option. The per diem was created to help cover expenses for employees who must work on-site, e.g., extra cost of transportation, food, or other expenses, along with other challenges related to coming to work during the crisis.*
- *In recognition that 2020 was an unusual year, and it was difficult for some employees to use their allotted paid time off by the end of the year, RBC allowed employees to carry over up to 10 days of PTO instead of five at the end of the year.*
- *Covered Doctor-On-Demand virtual visits at 100%. This enabled employees to visit a doctor without leaving home.*
- *Free, confidential support for stress, depression and other concerns for all RBC employees and their family members (ages 13+)*
- *Covid-19 testing covered 100% for RBC medical plan participants.*
- *Compensation continuity for employees working reduced hours because of childcare obligations and employees whose job could not be performed remotely.*

Community America, #1 Best Place to Work in Kansas City, 2020 (Financial Services) *

"Enhanced its parental leave benefits to four weeks of paid time off. Offers a new student loan assistance plan that provides monthly contributions to employee student loans to support faster payoff. The company hosted a virtual wellness fair that provided 21 hours of wellness learning and engagement. It also added mental health text therapy. Medical, dental, vision, life and disability insurance are expected, as is paid time off, a 401(k) and a wellness program. Above-and-beyond perks include a personal life coach, mental well-being benefits, free yoga classes, flexible and remote work, paid parental leave, paid volunteer time, a wellness stipend, donation matching, profit sharing, on-site fitness center, education assistance, mortgage and personal loan discounts, and employee gifts."

Alston & Bird, #3 Best Place to Work in Los Angeles, 2020 (Law firm) *

"Alston & Bird also prioritizes employee health. The firm offers a wellness program that encourages employees to focus on their health while earning discounts on insurance premiums. The firm's wellness committee also hosts daily exercise classes during the shelter-in-place period. Alston & Bird also provides all employees with child and elder care assistance through Bright Horizons. Employees also have access to college coaches, tutoring, test prep, and webinars and resources on parenting, education, and work/life integration."

Supreme Lending, #1 Medium-Size Best Place to Work in Atlanta

Most employees of the 10-year-old mortgage company started working from home during the economic shutdown of Spring, 2020 — mastering the art of Zoom and other teleconferencing apps. "When we do come back, we're pretty confident that we're going to have to adapt and allow some of our people to work virtually because some of them, frankly, now that they've gone virtual, like it that way," Operating Partner, Pat Flood said, adding that employees have discovered the working-from-home perks of no traffic, smaller dry-cleaning bills, and more time with family.

The company has an Associates' Emergency Fund to help employees facing unexpected financial burdens. Employees also have flexible hours, receive incentive pay for exceptional performance and commit to charitable giving. In 2020, they donated more than $300,000 to worthy causes.

Southwest Airlines *had a choice to make regarding employees who were overly stressed and burned out. According to an article in Forbes: "First, its chief operating officer Mike Van de Ven issued a public apology to its employees, acknowledging that increased demand '[took] a toll on our operation and put a significant strain on all of you, and for that, I am sincerely sorry.' Second, Southwest announced a bigger change: It cut its schedule during the crucial final months of the year to accommodate what the airline's pilots and flight attendants have been saying."*

Balsam Hill, *(Purveyor of high-end artificial Christmas trees), decided to work more closely with all employees to tailor their schedules based on when they prefer to work. Because of the labor shortage brought on by the pandemic the company was competing to hire employees who have the choice of working whenever they want to work. Said Kendra Gould, senior retail strategist for the company, "Now it's more about what do you need as an employee and how we can make you happy." Balsam Hill is just one of many employers who have listened and responded to their hourly employees who have been asking how they can get the same work-life balance as their peers who work remotely.*

Interested in more stories about companies who are leading the way on this lens? Check out award-winning companies in the "healthiest **employers**" category: <u>Healthiest Employers Blog</u>. They list six key values that support a healthy workplace. For each of your prospective employers see if you can find evidence of these factors that would help you determine the strength of this lens:

- Do they have a ***clear vision*** for becoming and maintaining a healthy workplace?
- Does their ***culture*** support a healthy workplace and where employees are engaged?
- Are there opportunities for employees to ***learn and grow*** in ways that support their health?
- Is there ***expertise*** available for programs that support a healthy workplace?
- Are there the ***right metrics*** in place that help an employer know if they're making progress and how to adjust course as necessary?
- Along with experts, are they ***using technology*** where appropriate to support these efforts?

Applying Insights from Successful Employers:

Some employers are committed to a healthier workplace for their associates as a way of engaging and retaining employees. Here are some practices for you to benchmark prospective employers you are considering:

- Did the prospective employer invest in employee well-being in difficult times, such as the recent pandemic?
- Does the prospective employer offer benefits that are of value to you? For example, if you are a working parent are their services meaningful to you?
- Does the company offer flexibility in benefits such as paid-time-off that will better meet your needs?
- Are the benefits offered keeping up with the changing needs of workers, such as offering elder care benefits?
- Is there support for employees who have difficulties, such as financial support or counseling?
- Importantly, does company leadership showcase the importance of a healthy workplace, including owning up to times when they may have not met the needs of employees?

1 Josh Bersin Research Report: The Definitive Guide for Wellbeing: The Healthy Organization

Lens #9:

Will I Find Honest, Caring, and Competent Leadership?

Stories of Three Who Were Disappointed:

Brenda Overhears a Disturbing Secret

Brenda took a job as Accounting Manager for a home furnishings store where she sat at a desk in the back office right next to the store owner/manager's desk. Brenda would write and mail all the checks except for a few that the boss would take to put in the mail himself. She thought that was curious, but she didn't question him. Brenda also filled out all government-related forms, except for the tax forms from the state department of revenue, which the boss made sure to keep in his desk. He insisted on filling them out and mailing them himself.

Because she couldn't help overhearing the boss making and receiving phone calls, Brenda would occasionally hear the boss talking to representatives from the state revenue department. He would turn away and lower his voice when those calls came in, but she could still hear most of what he was saying. She began to realize that he was reporting sales totals to them that were far less than the actual numbers. That's when she realized she needed to get out. As accounting manager, she was aware that she could be drawn into legal trouble herself. She began looking for another job and resigned within a few weeks.

Annie: The Head of the Fish…

Annie was excited about joining this emerging nonprofit. Yes, it was outside her industry, but the opportunity to build something from scratch was what she felt was a next great step in her career. Her skills were a great fit for the job, and she loved the team to which she was assigned.

The founder of the nonprofit was, however, another matter. She had been warned by two friends that the founder could be difficult to work with. One of her future coworkers even mentioned during interviews that the founder was "egotistical, to the point of narcissistic", and communicated in ways most would consider "demeaning". Annie ignored the feedback, thinking that the opportunity to grow and do something meaningful for a cause she believed in would win the day. She was wrong.

Within the first few months it was clear the founder was not a person with whom Annie could develop a trusting, productive relationship. She stuck it out for a year but returned to her former profession with an employer who offered meaningful work and a respectful culture.

Annie reflected on the experience: "A friend I confided in, who happens to be a biologist, said 'the fish rots from the head down.' In this case, that was sadly true." There was a serious lack of trust and terrible communication from leadership down to managers and line level employees.

Marshall: The Commitment That Wasn't

Marshall had built a strong reputation in his city for launching new initiatives to attract businesses to relocate and start up there. His enthusiasm, strategic approach, and sales ability had caught the attention of several business leaders, including a member of the board of a local engineering firm. The board member invited Marshall to join the firm, touting its commitment to building revenues with a new, more strategic approach to client acquisition and a desire to build a more transparent, employee-focused culture. Marshall accepted the job, along with a position on the company's board, and immediately set about to train regional managers in more effective sales techniques. He saw his mission as being a culture change agent to help the firm reach its very ambitious new revenue goal.

However, after a few weeks in his new role, upon return from a three-day vacation, Marshall was told he was being taken off the firm's board. This was the first sign that the company was not really committed to the vision portrayed on its website or in Marshall's job interviews. He was also becoming more aware with each passing week that the firm was not truly interested in changing its secretive, misogynistic, good old boy, seat-of-the-pants culture. The final straw came when a board member fired the assistant Marshall had hired without even letting him know in advance.

Marshall realized later that he was brought in as a vehicle to attract top talent and that the company had used the promise of culture change as the lure to bring him on board. He regrets not getting more input from people in the community who were familiar with the firm's culture prior to taking the job. Still, he learned quite a bit about the industry during his tenure there and he has parlayed that experience into subsequent assignments and sales successes.

Each of us must be useful to our employer and, hopefully, are valued for our skills, interests, and abilities. But there is a line that can be crossed and, when it is, we feel betrayed and devalued.

Employees Weigh in on Senior Leadership--Pro and Con

The conventional wisdom that "people join companies, but they leave managers" is true, but it's only partly true. People often leave employers because of the senior executive team, the cultures they create, and the examples they set for lower-level managers.

Witness the following **negative comments** from employee surveys we have collected in our research:

- *"Management isn't listening to employee concerns regarding the climate in the workplace, and the difficulty discussing problems with management."*
- *"There is a lack of leadership and accountability. I believe the leadership is deceptive and not ethical."*
- *"I'm a little nervous about the direction of the company. Our last product launch was a bust and no one took responsibility for it."*
- *"Senior leaders are completely and utterly unknown, unseen, uncaring, unconcerned, and unapproachable."*
- *"The leadership should give us more meetings/talks among all of us (all-company meetings) so that we can see how we are doing as a company, etc."*
- *"Improve transparency on what our vision is--making more money is not a vision. We need to know what we are trying to accomplish on a large scale, and how everything we do rolls up to that greater objective."*

On the other hand, we have found many **positive comments** such as these from employees who were happy with senior leadership:

- *"My owner is the best person I have ever worked for. He is not like other owners. He doesn't just show up and do nothing. He is there every day busting his butt like the rest of us. He doesn't care what job needs done; he will do it! He is amazing. And I would never want to work for someone else."*
- *"Our fearless leader and CEO is doing an amazing job. He is brilliant, has integrity, and never loses perspective of the work and the staff is doing and what they are asked to do. He welcomes feedback, responds to emails, and visits patients in the hospital on a*

regular basis. We love our CEO and I personally feel fortunate to be a part of this organization."

- *"I've worked in environments where I didn't entirely trust the CEO and management, which is why working here is so refreshing. I really believe that the management team has a lot of integrity and is genuine. The CEO is a focused, inspirational leader."*
- *"I began researching the company six months ago. I was impressed when I found direct phone numbers to the CEO and senior management team listed clearly on the website. Only a handful of companies have enough confidence in their quality of service to do that."*
- *"Our CEO typically schedules an off-site breakfast called 'How to Make This Company a Better Place to Work' at the beginning of every year. She invites small groups of employees from different areas to give open feedback on how things could be better, takes copious notes, and posts action items on the intranet."*

**Did the "Great Resignation" Lead You to Reassess
What you Expect from Senior Leaders?
Are they "just out for a walk"?**

Management guru Peter Drucker said, "a leader without followers is just a person out for a walk."

In the aftermath of the great resignation more of us are seeing leaders who are "just out for a walk." Avoid those who, during crisis, have shown themselves to be disinterested in the welfare of their associates, suppliers, and customers.

But there are leaders whose actions have shown them to be inspiring and committed, leading with compassion, clarity, and courage.

Find those leaders.

Inspiring, competent leadership has always been an important lens for evaluating prospective employers, but a cloudy or broken lens in these challenging times will likely lead to misery.

What Senior Leaders Do that Employees Find Demotivating and Disengaging

As we read and categorized exit survey comments about senior leaders, we noticed several definitive issues where employee expectations of senior leadership are not met:

- Basic Lack of Trust and Integrity
- Isolated, Unapproachable, and Out of Touch with Workers' Day-to-Day Reality
- Greed and Excessive Self-Interest
- Lack of Concern and Appreciation for Employees
- Lack of Trust and Respect for Employees

- Failure to Lead with Vision and Sound Strategy
- Inability to Execute Strategy and Manage Change
- Failure to Keep Employees Informed

Now would be a good time to reflect on these eight themes and highlight the ones that you would find the least acceptable. Recent workforce surveys of American workers show that it is unlikely you will join an employer where none of these themes are an issue.

Tony: A Story of Too Much Control and Too Little Trust

Tony accepted a VP position with a large firm owned and run by a billionaire CEO who, as it turned out, had an inordinate need for control and a very low level of trust. "He had installed a biometric clock for workers to check in and out via fingerprint recognition, yet on top of that he had a camera to watch and record them. Most companies let employees take the day off or let employees go home early the day before Christmas, but the CEO decided that he would allow only 50 percent of the workforce to go home early. He would walk around watching people to make sure they were doing their jobs. He actually went around pointing to people who could go home and those who couldn't. It was crazy. And he thought everyone was trying to cheat him out of money. I had to drive an hour and a half to and from work and yet he wouldn't pay for me to get a fast-track sticker for my car. He would refuse to pay vendors, forcing them to take him to court, then he would claim they had done a horrible job and hope the judge would rule he could pay them half of what they were owed."

What Research Tells Us About Trust in Leaders

For most workers, the trust issue is of paramount concern and the news is not good:

- Only 37% of global respondents rated CEOs to be sufficiently credible (2017 <u>Edelman Trust Barometer</u> survey)
- A lack of trust is a significant threat to an organization's ability to grow, according to more than half of the CEOs surveyed by PwC in 2016.

Effective leadership is largely about establishing trust. One-way leaders build trust is to communicate directly to employees. According to research by BI WORLDWIDE:

- Employees who reported that leaders were communicating directly to them were more engaged. More importantly, employees who felt listened to by leaders were even more engaged and inspired. Leaders who are open and transparent inspire more from employees.
- When employees feel a sense of both intrinsic and extrinsic motivation, they are more likely to report that they see their leaders as transparent.
- Employees who don't see their leaders as open and transparent are less likely to see their pay as fair.

Such survey data suggests that you need to do some detective work, especially if you have decided that quality of senior leadership is among your top criteria for finding your best-fit employer. Our opinion is that senior leadership should be near the top of every jobseeker's list because it dramatically impacts what managers do and all the lenses we have covered.

Don Moves Across the Country Only to Feel Out of Place

Don wasn't looking to move 3,000 miles to take an executive position with a west coast manufacturing company, but the 30 percent pay increase and moving expenses to a warmer climate were too attractive to resist. The only problem was that after making the move and starting the new job, Don realized it wasn't a good fit. "The other members of the leadership team, most of whom had been promoted from jobs on the factory floor, were relatively uneducated and unprofessional. They resisted the investments I asked for in my area, they didn't think strategically, and they didn't care much about treating the workers well. In other words, I realized quickly they weren't going to appreciate my management approach and that I didn't fit in or belong there."

Don resigned after only six months to take another senior job in a nearby location.

Look Through the Glassdoor

Glassdoor.com reports annually on the companies with the highest CEO ratings by employees who have reviewed the companies where they work. Glassdoor confirms that trust in senior leadership consistently ranks as one of the top factors that contribute to an employee's satisfaction.

Each year Glassdoor takes a close look at thousands of employee reviews on its platform to come up with its list of the <u>Top 100 CEOs in the U. S</u>.

To be considered for its list of the Top 100 CEOs in the U.S., companies must have 1,000 or more employees and receive at least 100 company annual reviews, including CEO approval ratings and senior management ratings. Small and medium-sized companies, those with less than 1,000 employees, must receive at least 35 company reviews during the year. Among the roughly **900,000** employers reviewed in a recent year, Glassdoor found **the average CEO approval rating was 69%.** Compare that number to **98%** for the top ten and you begin to appreciate what a remarkable achievement it is to achieve this distinction based on *anonymous* employee comments!

In reading excerpts from employee reviews, two of the most common themes that showed up were <u>*caring about employees*</u> and <u>*serving both employees and customers*</u>. These are the same two characteristics that we identified that described the CEOs that scored highest in our analysis of *Best Place to Work* survey data for our previous book, *Re-Engage*.

Most people will never have the privilege of working at an organization that is led by CEOs as beloved by its employees as these. You can increase your chances of being so lucky by following the guidelines below:

Do Your Due Diligence

So, what can you do to find out about the senior leadership team at the employers you are thinking of approaching or have already contacted?

Here are a few actions you can and should take:

- Ask your contacts what they know about the organization and its leaders, especially the leaders in the functional area where you would work.
- Look for people on LinkedIn who work there or have worked there in the past.
- Read the comments that past and current employees have made about the organization on Glassdoor.com.
- Do a Google search of the Best Places to Work in your city or the location where you are thinking of relocating.
- Do a Google search of the employers on your target list and search its leaders by name. Find out who is on their board of directors and ask your contacts if they know anything about them. Read everything you can find about your target employers.
- During interviews, ask about the leadership team's vision, business strategy, and the kind of workplace culture they are building.

Liz: Confronting a Culture of Rigid Incompetence

With over 25 years of experience managing major events in cities all over the U.S., Liz was excited about starting her new job as an events manager with a newly built state-of-the-art convention center. She had been asked by one of the facility administrators to apply for the position because, as she was told, they wanted someone with experience who could make decisions. But within days Liz began to see that some of her peers were unqualified for the jobs they held. Security and Parking were placed under the direction of someone with only a background in parking and was clearly not experienced with public assembly or security.

Liz had been trained early in her career to adhere to national fire codes and be involved closely with city fire marshals' inspection processes that give authorization for public events. But, when she inquired about the fire marshal's involvement in an upcoming event, she was shocked when the administrator responded, "If the fire marshal is here, there's a problem." As time passed, she witnessed repeated fire code violations.

Later Liz discovered that the four other event managers, all of whom had less experience than she did, were paid more than she was. Liz was often met with a "stay in your lane" response when approaching the organizations' administrators with what, in her experience, were serious organizational, operational and safety concerns.

The final insult came when she received a security proposal for a non-profit fund-raising event that was 33% over their budgeted funds for security, based on past years' security costs, with no justification for the increase. Liz felt a professional obligation to explain to her client why the security budget had been hiked to such an extent. Liz took up the issue with the security director who agreed with her concerns, but she was overruled by the facility administrator without explanation.

Liz submitted her resignation shortly thereafter. It had become clear to her that the source of all the issues was the lax, yet over-controlling and unfair culture that had been cultivated by the senior leaders.

After You're Hired: What You Can Do

Once you've checked out the senior team and have been reassured and hired, remember that it is your responsibility to be a good follower. Among the ways you can have a positive impact and help senior leaders achieve their goals for the organization (and ultimately your goals) are these:

- Complete all employee surveys and respond honestly to each question. Point out how the actions of senior leaders may not match their words and professed values. Be specific about pointing out instances of management behavior that have created distrust or caused you and other employees to lose confidence.
- Speak up in meetings and express your opinions and convictions thoughtfully and firmly.
- If you are asked to take part in something unethical, dishonest, or otherwise counter to the organization's stated values, refuse to go along, report it to a superior, or be prepared to resign.
- Be willing to take the risk of counseling your superiors against taking an action and will damage the organization's reputation.
- When a leader or manager puts trust and confidence in you by giving you the freedom to do the job without continuous oversight, be prepared to take the initiative.
- Show that you are interested in having an "ownership mentality." Learn how the business makes money and what you can do to make it more profitable and perhaps share more in that profitability.
- Earn your manager's trust by constantly looking for ways to take the initiative to meet customers' needs by improving your own skills so that managers will trust you to handle new challenges.
- Give new leaders the benefit of the doubt. Give them time to communicate their new vision and begin to execute it before judging them to be unworthy of being followed.
- If you feel called to be a leader yourself, resolve to do everything in your power to gain and keep the trust and confidence of your team.

Our Expert Panelists Share Their Perspectives on Senior Leadership:

Ed Baldwin: *"We know that 'the fish rots from the head down.' The CEO sets the tone for the whole culture, so I've always felt it was important to check them out before interviewing. I once had an interview with a CEO where I had looked up the company on GlassDoor.com beforehand, and I saw what low scores and uncomplimentary comments they had. So, at one point in the interview, I asked him about the low scores. Instead of explaining why the scores might be low, he became very defensive and resistant to discussing the subject of the company's culture. I knew right then that I was not pursuing the job further. I dodged a bullet by being real with the boss. If you're not comfortable being challenged, I don't want to work for you."*

Rick Beyer: *"Walk in the shoes of your leaders. Give leaders the benefit of the doubt. Attempt to understand the reasons for behavior that may be of concern to you. Forgive leaders for perceived shortcomings. Act in a trustworthy manner. Speak up in a constructive way. Answer honestly on employee surveys. Model the type of behavior you expect. Perform well and become highly valued. Lead well yourself and earn confidence in the job performed. Act justly, love mercy, walk humbly."*

Gary Bolles: *"A warning sign to me is when I hear people in an organization say, 'Leadership said….' Using leadership as a noun suggests that leadership is a black box of decision making and not particularly open to input. Look for the opposite. I also recommend looking at the LinkedIn profiles of the senior leadership team to see how psychologically diverse it is. Are they geographically diverse as well? Judging by their backgrounds, have they valued their own growth and development in their careers and are they committed to growth for all team members?"*

Dennis Boyer: *"You can tell a lot about the culture that senior leaders have built by carefully observing non-verbal behavior during the interview process. Do they meticulously handle details of setting up your interview, return calls promptly, help with directions and travel plans, welcome you warmly when you arrive, treat you with courtesy, punctuality, and professionalism? Look at the body language and eye contact of everyone you meet. Just know that you'll find differences in different industries--hospitality vs. technology, for example, or mature companies vs. start-ups."*

Mark Ernst: *"Ask how long the senior leadership team has been there. Has there been recent turnover at the senior level and why? How long has it been since the last reorganization? What happened to your predecessor in the job? How often does the CEO hold town halls with employees? Does the CEO communicate frequently enough to keep everyone informed? Senior leaders set the tone in the organization. Did the company lose money while the CEO continued to get bigger paydays? If it is a public company, check their quarterly and annual reports."*

"In any event, Google the company to see what has been written about them. When you are in the lobby waiting to be interviewed, what do you see? If you see staff diversity, it says something about the senior team. Do employees seem friendly or grim-faced? Are people running around like chickens with their heads cut off? How do senior leaders treat the

receptionist? I was happy to see a CEO spend a few minutes just chatting pleasantly with the receptionist as I waited. That told me a lot about him."

Andrea Hendricks: *"Find a company where leaders value diversity. What's great about diverse perspectives or diverse ideas is that you need to develop skills to deal with a more diverse organization. Good leaders do that."*

Ann Maltese: *"Senior leaders need to be more vulnerable, authentic, and transparent during tough times. The best ones did this during the pandemic. We did a survey for a company with 2,000+ employees and several hundred of them called out the CEO by name for how well he led the organization during Covid. He held weekly town halls to listen to what employees needed and he responded."*

Lynne Nelleman: *"You may have good reason to lose trust and confidence in senior management. You may need to leave. I live by three rules in the workplace. One, don't let the bad guys get you down. Two, don't become one of them by abusing or misusing those with whom you work: if you do, they win, and you've lost. And three, trivial as it may seem, send 'thank you' notes to at least two colleagues who have helped and/or supported you every week. I'm a churchgoer and I truly believe 'it's better to give than to receive' as the Bible says. Have your child 'intern' at your home office and demonstrate to them the qualities you wish you'd see in your senior managers. Be what they are not with your child, your spouse/parents, your friends."*

Alice Peterson: *"I've had almost 25 years' experience advising and serving on corporate boards and I've observed and experienced a wide range of cultures, boards of directors, and senior leadership teams. No senior leader or boss can be any better than its board of directors. My advice to job seekers is to visit the organization's website and read its stated values. Then, during interviews ask how each of the values translates into practice.*

"All too often, mission and values statements are expensive wallpaper. If the prospective leaders and other interviewers cannot give convincing examples of how the company is living each of its values, then you should probably think twice about going to work for them. It also reflects well on the job seeker that they have even given thought to asking such a question.

"Give a great deal of thought to the kind of workplace that would be the best fit for you. Imagine your best future boss. Imagine possible real-world issues and conflicts that might arise and how you would like the ideal company to respond. When meeting with different team members at a prospective employer, pose a scenario and ask how the company might handle it. It's like reverse behavioral interviewing. You might ask them to tell you about an ethical challenge that has come up and how they addressed it. If they say they can't think of one or that they've never had an ethical challenge, that's a warning sign.

"Prepare a list of other situations to ask about, such as how they might handle a situation that has arisen for many employees during the pandemic. How do they respond when an employee who normally works onsite needs to be home with family as a caregiver during protracted periods? It's even better to ask a third party who knows the culture, if possible."

Steve Puente: *"Check out what current and past employees have to say on Glassdoor.com and Indeed.com. Ask the people in your network and via LinkedIn. The CEO drives the culture. So, if you see a one-star rating for culture on Glassdoor, that's a bad sign. Beware of employers whose CEO's first instinct was to start laying people off after missing their number by a nickel."*

Gordon Smith: *"Be aware that senior leadership in most organizations turns over every three or four years. It happened to me twice. Know the politics at the senior level. You can learn a few things on Glassdoor.com. Before getting hired try to get plugged in so you know what's happening among the senior team if you can, especially the culture they are creating and their business strategy. Put your business hat on."*

Applying Insights from Our Experts:

Our experts know that effective senior leadership is an important lens for you to consider for prospective employers. Consider:

- What do you know about the CEO/Owner and the current leadership team of a prospective employer? What do you know about their reputation and how they lead the organization?
- What do social media sites say about the leadership of a prospective employer? Take into consideration that social media sites can be biased, but it is one additional data point to review.
- What is the diversity of the leadership team? How does their current standing align with your values?
- If there is an independent board of directors, what do the actions and makeup of the board tell you about the prospective employer?
- As you are getting a sense of the leadership of the organization, think about possible challenges the organization may face in the next one to three years. Based on what you understand about their past performance, can you get a sense of how they will react to future challenges?

Employers With a Reputation for Caring, Competent, and Trustworthy Senior Leaders:

Gravity Payments CEO, Dan Price slashed his $1.1 million pay package in 2015 to $70,000 so that he could fund a minimum $70,000 yearly "minimum wage" for all 130 of his employees. He was heavily criticized for the move at the time and lost clients who thought the salary hike would cause their rates to rise. Instead, the company's revenues tripled, employee head count doubled, turnover decreased by 50%, and employee home ownership increased ten-fold. The Harvard Business School now features a case study about Gravity's success. Price says, "Money buys happiness when it gets you out of poverty, but not when it gets you from well-off to very well-off."

Adobe's CEO, Shantanu Narayen ranks among Glassdoor's most beloved CEOs in America for building and sustaining a culture that values employee wellbeing. Employees get company-sponsored childcare, summer and winter breaks, wellness dollars up to $600, four weeks of sabbaticals after five years, infertility benefits up to $25,000, parental leave up to 26 weeks paid, 1:1 coaching for employees' children considering college, and educational reimbursement up to $10,000 a year.

The Brain Trust CEO, Sherry Stewart Deutschmann, founded the collective of women-owned businesses aimed at accelerating their growth. The firm has grown nearly 500% over the last three years. Because she felt unheard and unimportant while she worked as a dedicated employee earlier in her career, Deutschmann earns the loyalty and engagement of her staff by giving each Brain Trust team member 10% of the profit, giving total access to financial information, and granting phantom stock so if the company sells, team members will receive a chunk of the cash. Once a week she invites an employee to lunch and listens to their future aspirations and what they think the company can do differently. Deutschmann has authored the book, *Lunch with Lucy: Maximizing Profits by Investing in Your People.*

Weigh and Decide

Kudos for reaching this point in the process! You have looked through all the lenses and made the time and effort to reflect on how meaningful each of them is to you. You may have even changed your mind in the process, which is not unusual. For example, perhaps you now believe senior leadership is more important to your happiness at your next employer than you previously thought or that coaching and feedback is less important, or vice versa.

If you are fortunate enough to have a job offer at this point, or you expect to receive one, our Decision Grid will help you evaluate the job and employer based on your "must-have" needs and preferences. This is the preferred way to approach your decision and it is far more useful and enlightening than simply making a list of pros and cons. Even if you are not expecting or entertaining a job offer at this point, you will find that revisiting what you need from an employer to be a helpful exercise. If you are currently employed, for comparison purposes we recommend you evaluate your current employer along with other options on the decision grid.

Instructions: Turn back to Lens #1 where you listed your 20 "Must-Have" work-life needs/preferences and re-enter them on the Decision Grid below, keeping in mind that, having had the benefit of considering the seven reasons employees leave, you may choose to rank them differently now. You may even decide to delete one or two of your preferences from your list and add new ones in their place.

Do list them in order based on their importance to you now. The prioritization process will make it clear what you are less willing and more willing to trade off. This may also prove useful as you begin the process of negotiating compensation, benefits, and working conditions with your next employer.

Label each option (A, B, C, etc.) with the name of the prospective employer (or you may want to list self-employment as an option), then write in a number 1-10 (10 being best) to reflect the degree to which you believe each option meets each of your must-have needs. Bear in mind that you may still not know enough about how well the employer option meets a given need you have listed. If that is the case, you have more homework to do, so simply leave those boxes blank or pencil in a question mark.

After rating each employer on each of your needs, add up the points. The option with the highest point total is most likely to be your preferred option. As you gather more information about how each option meets your needs, you may change your ratings. So, use a pencil with an eraser!

YOUR DECISION GRID

Your "Must-Have" Work-Life Needs	A____	B____	C____	D____	E____
1.					
2.					
3.					
4.					
5.					
6.					
7.					
8.]					
9.					
10.					
11.					
12.					
13.					

14.					
15.					
16.					
17.					
18.					
19.					
20.					
Totals					

Regardless of your score, listen to your intuition!

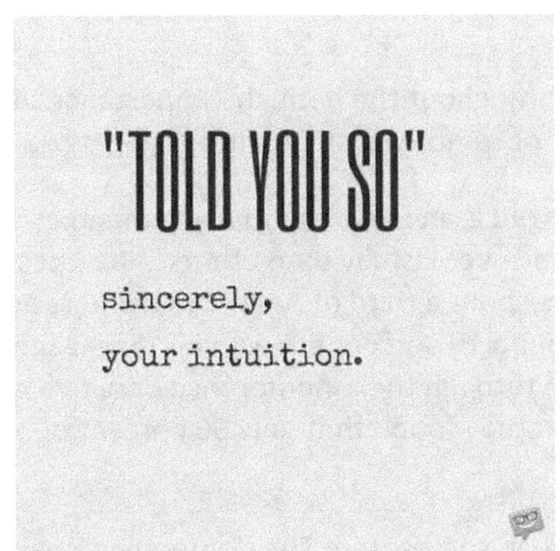

Keeping Yourself Engaged

We have been emphasizing throughout the book the importance of being in a work environment, whether onsite or remote, that you find engaging.

Keeping employees fully engaged is an ideal that many companies are actively pursuing, some much more enthusiastically and successfully than others. The latest survey from The Gallup Organization reveals that only about a third of American workers are engaged, while more than half are not engaged, and around 15 percent are actively disengaged, meaning they are actively undermining the organization through their indifference or active belligerence. So, what is employee engagement? One study found that only 66 percent of managers understand what employee engagement is.

The best definition we have seen comes from The Conference Board:

Employee Engagement is:

"A heightened emotional and intellectual connection that a team member has for his/her job, organization, manager, or coworkers that, in turn, influences him/her to apply additional discretionary effort to his/her work."

In other words, when you are fully engaged, you are choosing to work harder because you are getting something emotionally satisfying from the employer that makes you want to give back.

Our assumption is that you want to be a highly engaged employee who consistently achieves excellent results for the organization. In other words, you are not just concerned with "getting job satisfaction" but in also "giving satisfaction" to your employer and your colleagues, clients, or customers. If this really is your goal, think about your most recent job, or if you are employed, your current one. In that job, do you, or did you:

- Give your best effort every day, doing more than what is minimally expected?
- Take responsibility for and ownership of the organization's interests and objectives?
- Maintain an intense focus on customer service?
- Voice ideas for ways to improve things.
- Promote and model teamwork?

These are the typical actions of employees who are highly engaged, as documented by years of extensive research by The Gallup Organization. Most engaged employees are satisfied and successful in their careers because they are well-matched with their jobs and their employer's culture. There is a sense of "reciprocal commitment," meaning that they are willing to give their best because they are getting their needs met. This usually means they know themselves and get what they want and need from an employer. This is where many people fall short because knowing who we are and what we want is not so easy, as you may have realized while completing the exercises in Lens #1.

The research on employee turnover by Dr. Thomas Lee and his associates at the University of Washington has shown that in two-thirds of all voluntary decisions to leave, the employee experiences a "triggering or shocking event" --a straw that breaks the camel's back, so to speak, that causes them to immediately become disengaged and eventually leave. We have seen this pattern repeatedly in the stories we have shared throughout the pages of this book.

The following diagram shows *how* we gradually and sometimes suddenly become disengaged. Most of us start new jobs with some degree of enthusiasm until something happens that causes us to question our decision. Unless things improve, we may become disillusioned and consider quitting. Whether we begin to actively seek another job while working or not, we are most likely not giving our best effort during this time because we are in a state of disappointment and disengagement. We are likely to exhibit the warning signs shown below that can quickly become apparent to our manager and our immediate coworkers. Eventually, we may begin to look for a job elsewhere. Some quit and leave while others, as the joke goes, quit and <u>stay</u>, meaning they stay disengaged (aka "armchair attrition").

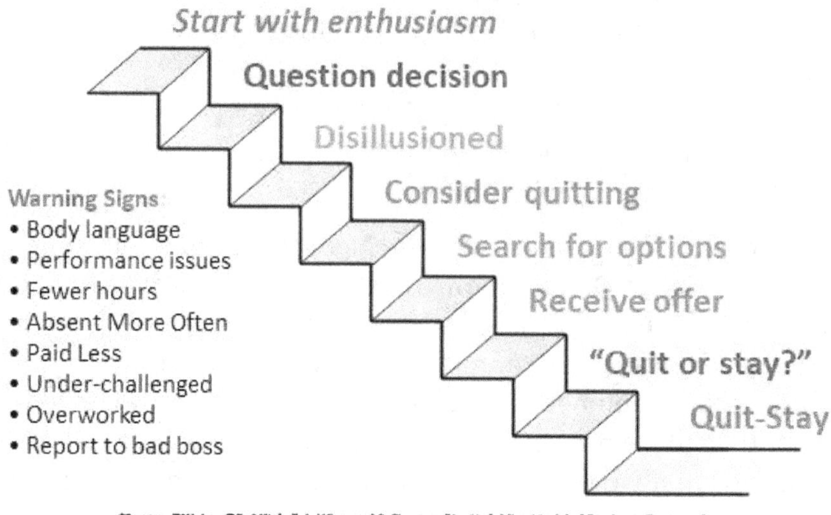

As mentioned previously, here are some examples of events that can trigger disengagement and decisions to leave:

- New manager
- No, or low, pay increase
- Disagreement with manager
- Conflict with a coworker
- Unexpectedly low performance rating
- Being passed over for promotion
- Being asked to do something unethical
- Realizing you are underpaid compared to others in the same job
- Being pressured to make an unreasonable family/personal sacrifice
- Being asked to perform a menial duty
- Petty and unreasonable enforcement of authority
- Incident of sexual harassment or racial discrimination
- Close colleague quits or is terminated

But with every triggering event comes a choice—do I react by giving less effort and leaving, or do I look for a way to stay engaged despite our disappointment?

Two of our survey respondents reported very disappointing day-one experiences in their new jobs:

"The worst part of my first day was not being asked to join anyone for lunch, so I ate alone."

Contrast that experience with a very different first-day experiences of another respondent:

"I was welcomed warmly and had someone with me the whole day. Multiple people told me how excited they were to see me and have me as a new part of the team."

On the first day in your next job your new employer may or may not do everything right to get you off on the right foot or set the tone for keeping you engaged. A friend of Mark's showed up for his first day, and no one at the company was expecting him. What job was he there to do? He was the new training specialist in charge of… you guessed it… new employee orientation!

You can't make this stuff up.

But suffice it to say, not every onboarding experience in a new job will go well.

But that doesn't change the truth that you are still in charge of your own engagement. The new hire who had to eat alone was faced with a choice--instead of eating alone on his first day and feeling sorry for himself, he could have introduced himself to someone in the company lunchroom and made friends with a new colleague.

Because only about one-fourth of the American workforce can be described as "fully engaged" (Gallup), many employers have begun training and evaluating managers on how to keep employees engaged. Years ago, a manager came up after one of our presentations and asked:

"Why does the responsibility for keeping employees engaged and motivated fall on the manager? Aren't employees responsible for keeping *themselves* engaged?"

Yes, of course they are. That's why we also conduct Self-Engagement workshops as well as training for managers on *Keeping Your Team Engaged*.

But it is true that in the process of training managers to be better at engaging their team members, many employers' engagement initiatives have overlooked self-engagement--the responsibility of all employees to keep *themselves* engaged.

So How Self-Engaged Are You?

We recommend you take a few minutes now to take the following Self-Engagement Assessment. If you are currently employed, respond based on your typical actions at work. If you are not currently employed, respond as you would have in your last job. Most importantly, be as honest with yourself as possible, which may be difficult because some of your typical actions at work may be hard for you to admit. As a reality check, ask someone who knows you well to look at your initial responses.

Self-Engagement Assessment (Self-scoring)

Instructions: Fill in the Points column as follows for each statement:
If you believe the statement **Always** described your behavior, score **2** points.
If you believe the statement **Usually** describes your behavior, score **1** point.
If you believe the statement **Sometimes** describes your behavior, score **0**.
If you believe the statement **Seldom** describes your behavior, score **-1** points.
If you believe the statement **Never** describes your behavior, score **-2** points.

Leadership   **Points**

	Points
I imagine myself in a leadership role and think about what I would do.	
In meetings with my manager and other leaders I assertively express my convictions and desires.	
Leaders trust me to take on challenges.	
I am a good follower—willing to give leaders the benefit of the doubt as they put their plans into action	
When I present my ideas to leaders, I am prepared with a specific plan for improvement and willing to help implement the plan.	

Manager   **Points**

	Points
I make sure I understand what results my manager expects of me.	
If I feel I am not getting the feedback and coaching I need, I ask for it.	
I have sought an active role in setting my own performance planning objectives with my manager and in evaluating my own performance.	
When there is a difficult issue to discuss with my manager, I do not hesitate to address it directly with him/her.	

Even when my manager is busy, I initiate communication when I need help or information.	

Teamwork   Points

I consistently demonstrate by my actions that I am open to different views and diverse perspectives.	
I willingly make sacrifices for the good of the team and to meet team goals.	
I commit to the decisions that are agreed on, even if I initially disagreed with them.	
I give and accept honest feedback in my interactions with other team members.	
When I have an issue to bring up with another team member, I do so directly rather than complain to others.	

Being Valued/Recognition   Points

I know what performance results and measures are valued by my manager.	
I have asked my manager what new skills and knowledge will make me more valuable to the organization.	

I have told my manager what form of recognition I most appreciate.	
When I feel I am "out-of-the-loop," I ask for more information.	
When I feel my input and ideas are not being sought, I find a way to make myself heard.	

Job Enrichment and Career Development   Points

I have worked hard to become very effective in my job.	
I recently learned something new that will help me at work.	
I have identified other jobs, roles, or assignments within the company that might be a good fit for my talents and interests.	
I have built relationships and increased my visibility throughout the organization.	
In the last three months I have initiated a conversation with my supervisor about how I could improve my performance.	

Personal Well Being   **Points**

In the last year I've done something (such as lose weight, quit smoking, started, or continued exercising) to improve my health.	
I have shared information with one or more coworkers about ways to improve their health and wellbeing.	
I manage stress at work so that it doesn't impact my productivity or health.	
When taking time away from work, such as a vacation, I easily put work behind me.	
When I don't have the information I need about benefits, I seek it out.	

General   **Points**

I constantly look for ways to exceed expectations.	
I'm always thinking of ways to improve things in my job.	
I volunteer for extra assignments and duties.	
I support and adapt to necessary changes in the organization.	
Even when things aren't going well, I give my best effort every day at work.	
When faced with adversity or difficult challenges I persist until the job is done.	

TOTAL POINTS ______

Fully Self-Engaged: (+54 to +72)
Mostly Self-Engaged: (+36 to +53)
Mostly Not Self-Engaged: (+35 to -53)
Not Self-Engaged (-54 to -72)

Bear in mind that the degree to which you are engaged is strongly influenced by how self-engaged you are, regardless of what your employer is doing to keep you engaged. Take special notice of the categories and particular items where your ratings are lower than others. For example, if your ratings in the Personal Well Being area are significantly lower than in others, that may simply confirm that you need to focus your energies on improving that aspect of your work life...IF it is a priority for you now. Many workers are willing to make sacrifices in this area (i.e., endure stress and work/life imbalance) to achieve other objectives, such as career advancement.

Keep in mind that how *self-engaged* you are may not always reflect how *engaged* you are overall. If your employer's culture, pay, benefits, and management practices are having a disengaging effect on you, you will almost certainly be less engaged than you might otherwise be as a result.

So, How Engaged is the American Workforce?

Based on the latest survey results by The Gallup Organization, the American workforce can be broken down into three categories. Here are definitions of each category:

Engaged

Highly productive, loyal, and psychologically committed to the organization.

Engaged employees:

- Give more discretionary effort, defined as the expenditure of effort solely at their own discretion (what we do because we want to, not because we must).
- Consistently exceed expectations, doing more than what is minimally expected.
- Take more responsibility for and ownership of the organization's interests and objectives.
- Receive better customer service ratings.
- Voice more ideas for ways to improve and innovate.
- Promote and model teamwork.
- Volunteer more for extra assignments and duties.
- Anticipate and adapt better to change and even facilitate change.
- Resist changes they see as harmful to the organization.
- Persist at difficult work over extended periods of time.
- Tolerate limited periods of lower work satisfaction.
- Speak well of the organization to friends and family.
- Are more likely to stay with the organization.

Not Engaged

May be productive and satisfied with salary, benefits, work relationships, and job stability, but not psychologically connected to the organization or finding much inherent satisfaction in the work.

The "Not Engaged" may often be described as:

- Doing the minimum expected of them.
- Reluctant to take risks or initiate.
- Fear of making mistakes.
- Uncomfortable with change.
- Keeping a low profile.
- Going along to get along.
- Feeling victimized, overwhelmed, and powerless.
- Comfortable to watch from the sidelines.
- Avoiding difficult conversations.
- Feeling disconnected from the organization.

Actively Disengaged

Physically present but disgruntled with their work situation and insist on sharing their unhappiness with their colleagues. They may even steal from the organization, spread rumors, undermine morale, and speak ill of their manager and the organization.
Their behavior is often characterized by:

- Always seeing the negatives.
- Criticizing ideas and solutions.
- Expressing frustration.
- Focusing on the past: "We tried this five years ago…."
- Arguing against change.
- Being oblivious to the consequences of their negativity.
- Bringing other people around to their perspective.

Many "not engaged" or "actively disengaged" employees have never been in a job that they would call satisfying or fulfilling. Some may have never thought of being "psychologically committed" to an organization as a realistic expectation because all they have ever known is bad bosses or toxic cultures. Millions of workers see their jobs as "just a paycheck" and don't emotionally invest in their jobs or their employers because they prefer or need to channel their energies into their lives outside of work. Others may say "I just really don't want to work that hard."

Because you have made it this far in this book and have completed the recommended exercises, we trust you want to be as fully engaged as you can be. That is why you have invested time and energy into acquiring the necessary self-insight and knowledge of the future employer.

How the Highly Engaged *Stay* Engaged and Successful

Keep in mind that even the most highly engaged employees can become temporarily or permanently disengaged by unexpected disruptive events, such as disagreements with a leader's decision or unreasonable demands on their personal lives. Engaged workers can become disengaged and vice versa. Staying engaged is a function of knowing yourself, monitoring the changing environment, staying resilient, and staying focused only on what you can control or influence.

Staying happy, successful (and mentally healthy) at work begins with knowing the difference between the things you can control and the things you cannot, as the following two diagrams show. The trick is to act on the things you can control, such as how hard you work, how much knowledge you acquire, how many new ideas you come up with, etc., and let go of the things you cannot control, such as the organization's structure, its policies, and benefits.

Personal Power Grid

	I Can Control	I Cannot Control
I Take Action	*Mastery*	*Ceaseless Striving*
I Take No Action	*Giving Up*	*Letting Go*

Personal Power – Getting What You Want

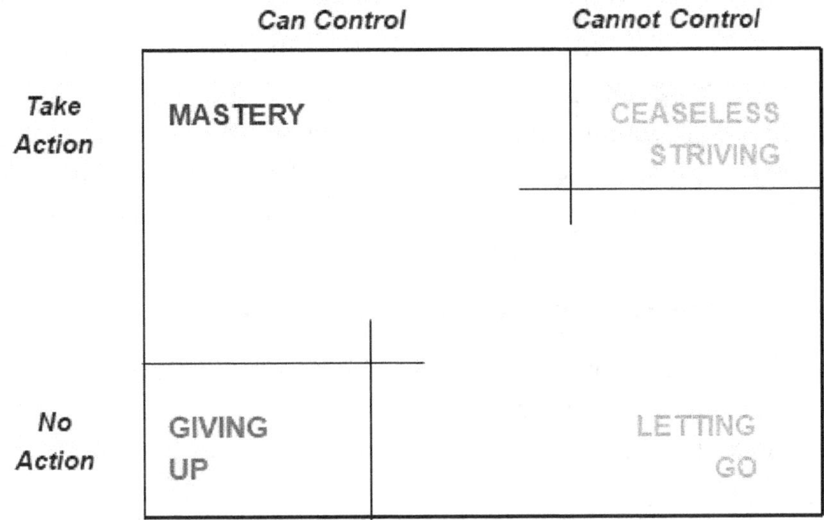

Adapted from Making Personal Changes by CD Scott and DT Jaffee, 1989

Jason Lets Go of Disappointment and Stays Engaged

After moving with his wife from Omaha to Minneapolis for his ad agency job there, Jason continued to do remote contract graphic design work for his Omaha employer while putting out feelers for a new job in his new city. One of Jason's contacts referred him to a design firm advertising for a Senior Design Director at another design firm, a position promising the opportunity to continue mentoring junior designers. Coaching others and managing the work process was the part of the job that Jason loved the most and it had comprised 90 percent of his activity at his former job as Associate Design Director. When he interviewed for the job, Jason was told that he would be expected to spend half his time doing brand development and the other half mentoring and managing.

That's not how things turned out. Instead, he was inundated with package design work and isolated at home because of the Coronavirus pandemic, leaving little time for interacting with coworkers. He was also disappointed that no branding assignments were forthcoming. Over the months he slowly realized that the firm's claims that they did branding work were more aspirational than actual. Jason blames himself for not asking one very important question during the interview process: "What kinds of projects do we predominantly work on as a firm?" which he admits is a question so basic he still can't believe he didn't ask it. Had he known he would be spending so much time just designing packaging, he would not have taken the job.

Still, Jason settled into the new job and, considering the alternative of seeking a different job in the Covid-ravaged economy, he focused on simply doing his job above expectations. He decided not to bring up his dissatisfaction with his manager. Instead, he decided to be a "good soldier", patient and grateful for the good aspects of the job—deepening his expertise and building a portfolio in packaging, working with interesting big-name clients with hefty budgets, and pulling down a decent salary. He decided to focus his energies on helping the company attract more branding work while keeping his eyes open for a better fit.

Jason chose to Master the situation and overcame his disappointment by taking responsibility for his failure to ask the right questions when he first took the job. He could have chosen to blame his employer for misleading him, playing the victim, and holding on to anger and resentment (Ceaseless Striving). Or, he could have Given Up on his goal of doing branding work. Instead, he recognized he had the Personal Power to help the agency get more of that work. He chose Mastery to stay engaged.

Habits of the Most Highly Engaged and Successful: A Checklist

What follows is a list of controllable actions that highly engaged employees tend to exhibit. Use it as a checklist of actions you can control that will make you more successful. As you read, *put a check next to the ones you feel you may need to improve*.

Highly engaged employees:

_____ Make sure to match their best talents to the job before taking it.

_____ Maintain a solid understanding of their manager's priorities and performance expectations.

_____ Learn all they can about the employer's history, products/services, policies, work processes, and the missions and objectives of various units, functions, and the organization.

_____ Understand and identify strongly with the employer's goals and objectives.

_____ Manage their time effectively by carving out uninterrupted time to work on the most important tasks and resisting the urge to complete the easiest to do or just the most urgent things on their to-do lists.

_____ Focus on results, not effort, and they know when it is often better to get the job done than to get the job done perfectly.

_____ Are willing to "go the extra mile" to get the job done even when it requires personal sacrifice. They push themselves to work extremely hard when the situation demands it.

_____ Continually add to their knowledge and area of expertise, including how to adopt the latest and most relevant technologies.

_____ Don't just drop problems on their boss' doorstep; they bring practical, well-thought-out solutions.

_____ Know when to speak and when to listen. When they speak, they are clear, concise, and assertive.

_____ Are willing to collaborate, tolerate differences, and make sacrifices for the good of the team.

_____ See what needs doing and take the initiative, often seeing better ways to do things.

_____ Are open to change and work to facilitate change when it is needed for the good of the organization.

_____ Manage stress and overall health through diet, exercise, and "constructive disengagement" (relaxing during time away from work).

_____ Plan out their next day the night before so they can put their mind at rest and sleep well.

_____ Seek out and build relationships with successful mentors.

_____ Admit their failures, learn from them, and take full responsibility for making sure that next time, things will turn out differently.

_____ Intensely focus on serving the needs of clients and customers.

_____ Maintain a sense of humor and have fun at work.

_____ Keep a healthy perspective, knowing that the universe doesn't revolve around them and their worries. They understand that if the boss doesn't pat them on the back every day, it's probably because he or she probably has other things on their mind. They don't expect perfection.

_____ Get to know their coworkers as people and learn about their personal lives and challenges.

_____ Remind themselves of all the things they are grateful for, and express appreciation for their coworkers.

_____ Have an "ownership mentality" (i.e., treat the company as if it were theirs), which leads them to make prudent decisions and recommendations about spending and other key issues.

_____ Are willing to bring bad news and uncomfortable information to the surface when not doing so would bring damage to the organization.

_____ Lead by example and inspire others to raise their level of performance.

_____ Demonstrate their value to their managers and, when asking for a raise, present their case based on the value they have created for the organization, not on their own needs.

If this sounds like the perfect employee, we must admit that it does. Very few, if any, employees, can check all the above. There is no such thing as a perfect employee just as there is no such thing as a perfect employer or a perfect boss.

Now may be a good time to go back to your list of Potential Derailers in Lens #1 and consider whether any issues you checked on that page may be holding you back from being as highly engaged and successful as you would like to be.

For more inspiration on staying engaged, check our recommended reading list in the back of the book.

Dorothy Gets Feedback and Adapts

As an African American convention events management professional, Dorothy had been frustrated with the lack of leadership opportunities at her previous employers. So, she was excited to be recruited by a company where 95 percent of the staff, including senior executives, were people of color. "I accepted the job expecting to be groomed for a senior executive position myself," she told us. "What I didn't expect was that the team I supervised would see me as intimidating or threatening when I began to make some changes."

"Someone on the team who wanted my job complained to HR and I found myself being the subject of 360-degree feedback. With the help of an outside consultant, I accepted that some of the tough feedback about me was valid--that I had not listened or been as inclusive as I could have been when I started the job. I looked inward and acknowledged my imperfections. But in the process, it became clear that some of the team's concerns about me were selfishly based on what they would personally lose, not on what was best for the organization. Over the next three years I brought in new staff, trained them, listened to them, gave them a voice in decisions that affected them, gave them travel opportunities, gave them lots of feedback, and gave them individual recognition at group meetings. I was there for eight great years before leaving to accept a senior executive position with another company."

"My style is to see something and say something. For example, I lived near the office and walked to work. I saw that the front of the building was dirty and hadn't been power-washed, so I mentioned it in an executive forum. The other team members had never noticed it because they all drove to work and came up on the elevator. Still, they reacted defensively when I brought it up. When you start a new job, you must pick your spots and be careful about pointing out too many things you want to change too soon."

Our Expert Panelists Share Their Thoughts on Keeping Yourself Engaged:

Ed Baldwin: "Believe that you really can be fully engaged at work. Also, think about your legacy. There was an executive at a company where I worked who, when he retired, could proudly and honestly say that there were 26 other VPs in the company that he had supported or mentored."

Rick Beyer: *"I believe we all want something more than a job, something bigger than ourselves. William H. Dunn, Sr. of J.E Dunn Construction Company, used to say, 'the only thing we do better than building buildings is building community.'" That is, service above self. Reciprocity nearly always occurs, and we discover that in the process of serving others our needs are fulfilled.*

"To stay engaged, assess gaps between what you expected and workplace realities. Reflect on what you have learned, then adapt to close those gaps while being the best employee you can be. Show how valuable you are. Err on the side of sticking with it to make things better. Analyze your relationship with managers, coworkers, and clients or customers. How can you get closer and build stronger relationships? There is so much focus on 'my needs not being met' these days

vs. choosing your own attitude and adapting. One of the last freedoms is to choose one's own attitude, regardless of the circumstances (see Victor Frankl's classic book, Man's Search for Meaning).

"Build a reputation as a highly effective employee. If the fit is not optimal, work up into a new better-fitting role or out to a better position in an organization where the fit is better. We cannot just run the other way when things do not go our way. Life does not commission" dryland sailors" (Charles Spurgeon). The exclusive pursuit of self-actualization can cause us to chase it away. Make the most of your circumstances. There are always unseen opportunities to make the best of it. Test your resilience.

"Life involves a series of transitions. We must learn the stages of transition and manage them: Reconcile, Reorient, and Recommit."

Appendix A:

Dealing with Bias
in the Job Search

Nia's Story: NOT WASTING HER PURPOSE

The recruiter seemed sincere: "Our sales organization doesn't reflect from a diversity perspective the diversity of our consumers. We consider this a problem. Join us." So, Nia said yes and became one of the first African American women in the sales organization of the company. The decision felt good at first. Her orientation offered her contact with the senior leaders of the company and the company training program provided her the insights she would need to go into the market confidently.

But the direct supervisor who was assigned to her seemed aloof. He wasn't that way with the other sellers on his team. And when she brought requests or problems from her customers it was clear that the support teams simply weren't as responsive to her requests as to her peers. Deadlines she was given were missed and promises not kept. She saw this as a reflection not only on the company but on her reputation.

Her parents told her they named her Nia because it meant "purpose", and she believed her purpose was to be in roles that weren't typically filled by African American women: "I'm willing to put myself out there and take the rejection you get in sales, but I'm not willing to take it from the people who should have my back. Selling is still my mission, my purpose, but just not here."

ARE YOU FEELING "THE GLARE"?

Dr. Donald O. Clifton, the grandfather of positive psychology, was at a client's national sales meeting. He heard people whispering about a man across the room. Although the man had on a nice sports coat and tie, he apparently had made a faux pas with his socks…

They were white.

Don found out later that the man with the white socks, although ridiculed, was an outstanding performer. In fact, his hecklers didn't know that later that day he was being honored as a top salesman at the meeting.

Don deemed his peers suffered from "glare," because, in this instance, they were judging this man wearing white socks which, of course, has absolutely no relationship to his productivity and success.

If Don were alive today, he wouldn't call it glare.

He would call it bias.

Too many of us will experience bias in the job search. It will have nothing to do with our ability to perform a job and be successful. This is the most heinous way we devalue others.

What the Research Tells Us About Bias Against Underrepresented Job Seekers

The most recent research from an organization called Matheson [1] provides insights into the challenges that job seekers from underrepresented communities face:

- 74% of underrepresented candidates see diversity potentially as a disadvantage in the hiring process.
- 62% of underrepresented job seekers report actively facing bias in the hiring process.
- 50% of underrepresented job seekers observed exclusionary language in job descriptions.
- 76% of underrepresented job seekers observed a lack of diversity on interview panels.

Dimensions of Bias

There are countless ways people experience bias, and the job search is just another one. Here is a list (not likely complete, sadly) of the ways job seekers have experienced bias:

- **Gender.** Our panelist **Lynne Nelleman** has been a leading voice in addressing the "glass ceiling", including a role on the President's Glass Ceiling Commission. Along with the lack of promotion opportunities is the wage gap, where women earn significantly less than men who have similar qualifications and experiences. Personal humiliation is common. In Lynne's case, she was asked how many people she had to sleep with to get to her role.

- **Age.** Our panelist **Bill Ellermeyer,** who was 83 at the time of our interview, had definite thoughts about ageism. *"It's real,"* he said. *"The key is to maintain your brain health by continuing to learn and staying mentally active. Stay passionate to stay energetic. I never use the "R" word--Retirement. It conjures up Old and Obsolete. I look at actors, William Shatner, and Clint Eastwood--both 90-year-olds with active ongoing career projects."*

- **Ethnicity.** One of the consequences of the systemic racism that has confounded the United States is the wage gap of African Americans. A recent study: In 2020, the typical full-time black worker earned about 20 percent less than a typical full-time white worker. And black men and women are far less likely than whites to have a job. So, the median earnings for black men in 2019 amounted to only 56 cents for every dollar earned by white men. The gap was wider than it was in 1970."[2] Other ethnic groups continue to face bias in the workplace. Recent increases in Asian-American hate crimes are, unfortunately, another example.

- **Disability.** Individuals with disabilities—physical, mental, or intellectual— in total comprise almost twenty percent of eligible workers [3]. Often first out of the workforce in an economic downturn and last back in, individuals with disabilities face many challenges in the workplace.

- **Gender Identity.** Individuals from the LGBT community make up approximately 4.5% of the workforce, and surveys indicate that most of this group believes that bias exists in the workplace.[4]

- **Religion/Faith Tradition.** Although against the law [5], many individuals suffer bias in the workplace because of their religion or choices regarding faith.

- **Hairstyles and Ethic Fashions.** Some workers, regardless of gender identification, report experiencing bias based on hair styles and fashions. This can be a particular challenge for African American women.[6]

- **Obesity.** Numerous studies have provided evidence that individuals who are obese experience bias, as obesity is often falsely equated with intelligence or competence. This bias may be more significant for women.[7]

- **Employment Status.** This is going to sound odd, but there is evidence that employers have a bias against the unemployed.[8] The research indicates employers may "think something is wrong" with individuals who are unemployed.

- **Refugees and Immigrants.** Regardless of citizenship status and laws prohibiting such practices [9], recent communities of refugees and immigrants often experience bias in the workplace.

- **Pregnancy.** Again, although codified as illegal [10] in the United States, women who are pregnant frequently report concerns of employer concerns regarding their pregnancy.

- **Prior Criminal History.** Individuals who have a criminal record may face bias. In some cases, an employer can make a case for not hiring a person with a criminal record [11]. For example, someone who has been convicted of a crime that involves cash may be precluded from working in a financial institution, although other opportunities are available.

- **Poverty**. Being impoverished can be a barrier to employment and, in that sense, forms a bias. As was noted on a social media comment: "I just told someone that some people are so poor, they can't afford to get jobs. He laughed. But I wasn't kidding. Gas money, childcare expenses, and lack of clothing to meet dress code requirements are often barriers for low-income individuals."

We have heard too many heartbreaking stories of people who experience bias in the workplace, who are not valued for their accomplishments or potential to be successful at a job:

"I'm forced to search for a job that allows for medical care and flexible hours because I'm trying to get through school and have a DUI that doesn't look good on a background check. Currently transferring to a new location to solve these problems but this happens at most stores and most managers are brainwashed into thinking they make "important" decisions and try to make their employees equally deluded."

On the other hand, many job seekers have found workplaces that are more welcoming:

"I wanted to have a job that accepts me as transgender, with benefits that have helped me achieve those goals. But it wouldn't have been possible without a 2nd job. This job recognized me as being trans and accepted me. There's absolutely no discrimination."

ALICE'S LESS-THAN-IDEAL EXPERIENCE

One of our panelists, Alice Peterson, had her own disappointing experience with a new employer. *"I took a job where I didn't yet know enough to be competent even though I had the title and the salary. I was fortunate that the company was looking to hire females at the time, but they were doing very little to help make women successful after bringing them on board. It was a culture known for backstabbing and not showing weakness. I suffered in silence in the beginning. I worked like a dog. I scrambled, brought work home, worked evenings and weekends."*

"Under-represented groups need the book you are writing," she believes. *"Employers may not have the skills or experience to include them. Many employers are making a big push to hire diverse candidates. One company said, 'we're going to have six black VPs by this time next year!' It was scary to hear that. It's just about numbers in some companies, with little thought about the long view and their longer-term inclusion. I haven't seen many employers be as effective at setting up buddy systems or mentoring processes to help these diverse new hires succeed."*

EVEN WORSE FOR SOME—WHEN BIASES INTERSECT

A study [12] was conducted (which has been replicated many times) that provides evidence of a level of bias which can be even more hurtful—it is called intersectionality. Here's the study:

Several thousand resumes were sent to employers across the United States. All the resumes were exactly the same except for one change—the first name listed on the resume. The resumes were sent out with four different first names: "Greg", "Emily", "Jamal" and "Lakisha".

That's it. Everything else on the resume—skills, background, employment, education—were the same. The researchers then waited to see how many inquiries were returned from each of the four groups.

Care to guess the results?

The "Greg" resume received the most, followed by "Emily", then "Jamal". Finishing last in terms of the number of resumes receiving requests was "Lakisha". Mind you, the mere suggestion of a name changed the response rate. "Jamal" is a name which is more common with African American men and "Lakisha" for African American women. But "Lakisha" had even less engagement than "Jamal", and this is evidence of the intersection of bias of two categories—ethnicity and gender—creating even more bias.

Intersectionality could be applied for other groups:

- An African American man who has a disability would likely suffer more bias.
- A Caucasian woman who identifies as lesbian would likely experience the bias of intersectionality.
- A Hispanic man who is an immigrant may be subject to the challenges of intersectionality.

If you have an intersection of two areas where there is historical bias, the road to a new job could be even more challenging. Later in the chapter we'll discuss strategies to moderate the bias you may experience.

THE PSYCHOLOGY OF UNCONSCIOUS BIAS

There is an emerging field called behavioral economics, which is defined as "studies of the effects of psychological, cognitive, emotional, cultural and social factors on the decisions of individuals and institutions and how those decisions vary from those implied by classical economic theory."[13] It is a field that didn't exist a few decades ago, but now these researchers are winning Nobel prizes.[14]

Behavioral Economics helps explain that we are all, in some way, biased. Here are some ways that may particularly impact your job search:

- **Similarity Bias**—we prefer what is like us over what is different. A hiring manager who is from an ethnic group may have a bias to hire others from the same ethnic group.
- **Expedience Bias**—we prefer to act quickly rather than take time. If a hiring manager has one candidate who may not be ideal but looks okay, they may choose or make an offer immediately rather than wait to source other candidates.
- **Experience Bias**—we take our perception to be the objective truth. A hiring manager may have a bias to hire only from a certain school, believing their training is the only source of qualified candidates.
- **Distance Bias**—we prefer what's closer over what's farther away. A hiring manager may have a bias toward a candidate who is willing to work at the office versus being remote.
- **Safety Bias**—we protect against loss more than we seek out gain. A hiring manager with a certain industry background may have a bias against hiring individuals who come from different industries, believing hiring someone from the same industry would be the "safer" choice.
- **Confirmation Bias**—we tend to look only at information that supports our prior beliefs or values. A hiring manager may have a bias in favor of hiring only men because of a belief that men have been the only candidates in the past that have been successful.

How can these biases impact our job search?

A hiring manager who is Caucasian may fall prey to similarity bias, where they prefer to hire employees of the same ethnicity. A human resources recruiter who has had success hiring from a particular school may have a bias toward prospective employees who have the same educational background, which would be evidence of experience bias.

We can't eliminate bias but being aware of them can help us conduct a more effective search.

WHERE DOES BIAS OCCUR IN THE HIRING PROCESS?

We've talked about groups who have experienced bias in the workplace, so let's turn our attention to the parts of the hiring process where bias may rear its ugly head-- what part of the hiring process can you find bias?

Every part.

We want to walk you through the hiring process and point out where it is possible for you to experience bias. Being aware of these moments may help you manage bias:

- **Benchmarking of Prior Employees.** There is a practice where a manager will think about a person who has been successful in a position, and this information is often used in developing the job description for the role. Although there can be value in this benchmarking, bias can arise when it eliminates individuals who may not fit the benchmarking but could still be successful in the role. This could eliminate some individuals who could be successful if considered.
- **Job Search Postings.** Numerous studies have shown that the language of job postings can create bias. A common example of bias can discourage women from applying for roles that have historically been male dominated.
- **Job Search Algorithms.** A chilling documentary called "Coded Bias" explores how bias is being built into the machine learning that drives many decisions, including algorithms in applicant tracking systems.
- **The Employment Application.** The actual job application could create bias. For example, a compelling study has been conducted which provides strong evidence that asking about prior salary history creates bias against women and African Americans. Be aware that in some states and local jurisdictions it is against the law for an employer to ask about prior salary history.
- **Resumes.** Information you have on your resume may signal to a hiring manager information which can create bias. If you put onto your resume that you graduated from high school in 1977, chances are that you are in your early sixties, information which form the basis of age discrimination.
- **Interviews.** There are several questions that are illegal for a prospective employer to ask, and there are additional questions that aren't illegal but still can create bias. For example, an interviewer who asks you "how did you get here today?" may have a bias against people, believe it or not, who use public transportation.
- **Pre-Employment Assessments.** It is not easy predicting who will be successful from a pool of job candidates, so employers will use various techniques to increase their chances. Testing prospective employees is one additional avenue. Many tests are designed in a way that they provide evidence that successfully predicts who will be successful in a job without having bias against legally protected classifications such as age, gender, and ethnicity. Having said that, some assessments are not designed to be used in the pre-employment process. One example is the Myers-Briggs Type Indicator. It

has many uses, including team building and career counseling such as we have described, but has never been validated for use in pre-employment.

● **Job Offer/Negotiating.** We have already discussed how asking about prior salary history on the job application can create bias, particularly against women and African Americans. If salary isn't reported on the job application, the bias can be raised in the final negotiations.

MODERATING BIAS: LOOK FOR A CULTURE OF INCLUSION

What do Berkley, California and Kalamazoo, Michigan have in common?

They were leaders in creating a more inclusive community and, in doing so, created a community that worked better for everyone.

What was this revolutionary change, one that helps an underrepresented community and helps everyone else?

The curb cut.

You know what a curb cut is, right? You've used them in airports and grocery stores and on street corners.

We didn't always have curb cuts, but in Kalamazoo and Berkley got out ahead and designed them to help folks with disabilities, specifically where the disability is mobility.

But here's the funny thing that happened-- over the years we've found that curb cuts can helps lots of us-- at the supermarket, airport, and the like.

Curb cuts were designed to help one underrepresented population but ended up helping everyone.

It turns out that efforts to build a culture that is more inclusive for underrepresented groups are also engaging for everyone.

A good culture is like a curb cut.

Over the past few years, BI WORLDWIDE has been studying the characteristics of an inclusive work culture. According to BIW's Managing Research Director, Amy Stern, there are several cultural factors which help people feel that their workplace is "for people like me"—a culture where employees feel included. These fortunate employees:

- Believe their jobs matter.

- Don't feel isolated.

- Are recognized when they do good work.

- Are confident they can fulfill their potential and grow with the organization.

• Trust leadership.

• Feel supported when they make mistakes.

• Have managers who make decisions in the employee's best interest.

• Feel everyone's ideas are taken seriously.

• Feel their leaders are open to different points of view.

If these factors are present, the culture is likely to be one that is engaging and inspiring for all, but if you are concerned about bias, you will want to assess how the culture of each prospective employer rates on these key factors.

If they don't have a curb cut culture at a prospective employer, it might be worth looking elsewhere.

Disability Doesn't Mean Inability: A Lesson for All Job Seekers

Mark was on the board of the directors of an agency that helped individuals with disabilities find employment. In one case the agency placed a young man on the autism spectrum at a car dealership. The young man could drive, so they assigned him to detailing cars for customers after they had been serviced.

Even though the young man had social challenges, he really enjoyed cleaning. He enjoyed it so much he would go the extra mile to make sure the car looked great, perhaps as good as new.

Customers loved him.

They would even wait in line, time they could have spent elsewhere, just so he could clean their car.

Find a workplace that will not only "put up" with who you are but will celebrate you.

Every bit of you.

MODERATING BIAS IN YOUR JOB SEARCH—ADVICE FROM OUR PANELISTS

Our panelists provide thoughtful and pertinent advice regarding bias:

Andrea Hendricks challenges all of us to think about our diversity and, in a sense, our own bias: *"All of us are diverse. In the workplace, it's about whether we have equality and fairness for all. One day I hope we can forget about these differences. In the meantime, it is a difficult problem to have to navigate."*

"If someone has experienced bias in the past, they have more homework to do to ensure the environment is safe and productive, not only through words but through their actions. And if they choose to go there then they can take up the call to help the organization and leave the place better than when they left it. While you're there you make it easier for those who will come after you."

Sherry Benjamins: After 30-plus years in executive search and career transition services, she switched the focus of her consulting work to facilitating mentoring groups and coaching young professionals. She holds focus groups and now meets regularly with groups of 8 - 15 Millennials in each. They describe their frustrating experiences with the hiring and on-boarding process. *"One young woman told the group about being hired as the only woman on the company's sales team consisting of men 20-30 years older. The company was looking to hire younger people, but they made no effort to mentor her or smooth her transition into the work environment and her new team. She did not feel included and quit after a few months."*

Benjamins offers timely advice to employers who are seeking a more inclusive workplace: Regarding the hiring of diverse candidates, *"The hiring manager needs to think through what would entice African Americans or any other minority to want to work here."*

Benjamins points to a couple of employers who are doing it right. Sparks and Honey, an ad agency in New York City, set up an internship program for people with 30 or more years of experience to mentor Millennials. Shutterfly, the San Francisco area marketer of photo books and cards, has gone so far as to require that 50% of candidates need to be people of color. *"This has forced them to think through how welcoming the culture would be."* She suggests that minority candidates ask about actual scenarios where current minority employees have been successful.

She points out that there are many new job openings for Chief Diversity Officer across the U.S. Candidates for these positions, she says, should ask what the desired outcome of implementing a major diversity initiative might be and what obstacles need to be overcome. Often, the diversity officer reports to HR instead of the CEO, and that might be a red flag. Is there an appropriate link to the business and how diversity goals transcend "hiring people of color?" She continues: *"It's OK to be curious in the job interview."*

"Getting hired is not just about your collected experience. In today's job market it's about knowing the organization and how your strengths can make a difference in the business. You must reinvent yourself to keep up with the pace of change."

Bill Holland: *"I have a simple philosophy about bias--it's not something I worry about. Just do the best you can. I was chief affirmative action officer at a large company headquarters back before that company had not yet integrated many of its cafeterias in the American South.   I just plowed ahead and did my best, knowing people had attitudes over which I had little control. It's popular now to believe that everyone needs to wear their red badge of courage, but some things are not going to change very quickly in some environments. Just be as informed as possible about a company's values before you take that job."*

Lynne Nelleman: *"I have had my own experience with workplace bias. I call it The Longest Hallway Handshake. The CEO was walking me around to meet some of the executives. While our tall, well-respected, genteel CEO proceeded down the hall, I shook the hand of one executive, and he blurted out 'How many men did you sleep with to get this job?' Can you see it in your mind's eye? I'm shaking this guy's hand. Our CEO is out of earshot range.*

"I tightened my grip somewhat, kept shaking this man's hand and replied 'you know… we'll need to work together. That's gonna be hard to do with what you just said. Zero. The answer is NONE! Our company is #27 on the Fortune 500 list. We're better than what just happened here.'"

I continued: "In the best of worlds, you might be trying to toughen me up. Helping me get ready if I have that question asked in a press conference. Maybe you have daughters, and you want to give them a good answer when they are asked that question. We're not talking about a 'good' answer. What you've said is rude, insulting, maybe illegal, and if it was asked of your wife or daughter you'd rush to her defense. "

"We kept shaking hands. I went on: 'In the worst of worlds, you said what you thought or tossed it out like a bar room taunt. You judged on gender. That's not a qualification for this job. My job is to… (mentioning two or three job requirements). And we both have the job of presenting this company in the best possible way, enhancing its reputation, meeting shareholder expectations, outperforming our competitors in the 21st century."

"His was a quick, short, and sincere apology. The longest handshake for each of us. Fortunately, no one else came down that hallway. My five-word response if sexually approached is, 'I'm flattered but not available.'"

"If something like this happens to a woman, my advice is to seek out that fella. Have a serious talk with him or his superior."

"I am the daughter of a mother who was director of the Girl Scouts in Michigan and a father who climbed the corporate ladder and wanted the same opportunity for women. I followed in their footsteps. It's still a white man's world. Fortunately, that's changing, but all too slowly, not

just for women, but for blacks, Asian-Americans, and those without college degrees. I chaired the Federal Glass Ceiling Commission, on report to Secretaries of Labor in both Republican and Democratic administrations. The data is irrefutably consistent and has been for decades. "

"After you start a new job, study the policies, procedures, and protocols of your employer. What are its stated employee, ethical and legal rights? I'm not suggesting you major in constitutional law. But if you see something, say something, to those who can change something. It might be to a colleague, supervisor, auditor, or human resource professional. I know this…there are as many realities as there are individualities. It's unmet expectations, the employee's or the employer's, that push you aside or out the door."

"Getting hired is never based simply on skill sets. We all face bias--yea or nay reactions to us based on gender, age, ethnicity, sexual identity, or personality. The color of your skin or hair, the un-pronounceability of your name, your height, BMI or weight, the sound of your voice, how you dress, what and how you eat, your posture and manners, marital or parental status, whether you are or are not a team player, whether you have molded yourself through sports, avocations, travels, music, arts, or charity. It's never just about you. It's about them--those who can hire or fire and favor those who will be the best 'fit' in terms of culture, salary expectation, determination, or aspiration."

"My advice? Don't drop out of the race. If it's not perceived as a 'fit' for them, it won't be a 'fit' for you. What's your next 'best step?' Learn from every no and every yes. It's your response that will make or break your chances of getting that job.

Gordon Smith remarked that "If you believe age or long service is a hurdle, it will be." He advises: "Focus on your experience. Can you learn new tricks? Are you healthy? Show your energy. Talk about a new software program you just learned."

A final thought:

"We are each of us an endangered species. When we die, our species disappears with us. Nobody like us will ever exist again."

--Journalist Janet Malcolm, quoted in Artforum.com

Employers That Promote Diversity and Inclusion:

RBC Wealth Management, #1 Best Places to Work in Minneapolis-St. Paul, 2020* RBC maintains a focus on building a diverse workforce, an inclusive workplace, and diverse partnerships in the following ways:

- Ensuring that nondiscriminatory language is used in external job postings so that diverse candidates can see themselves in the role they are applying for.
- Employing inclusive recruiting guidelines that ask every hiring manager to interview at least one diverse candidate for all their posted roles.
- Proactively reaching out to diverse communities, including college campuses and organizations.
- Increasing its presence and sponsorship of diversity recruiting events for women, veterans, people of color, individuals with disabilities and LGBTQ candidates.
- Working more closely with our internal employee resource groups to encourage employee referrals.

HOK, #6 Best Place to Work in Los Angeles, 2020 (Architecture/Design) * HOK's Diversity Advisory Council, which is made up of volunteers from across the company's studios, reflects a rich diversity of age, gender, ethnicity, sexual orientation, experience, expertise and geography. The group's mission is to promote an inclusive work environment and help create a culture in which all HOK's people can thrive.

There are many employers who have been recognized for diversity. Below are two such programs. Use programs such as this as guides to employers who may be bit further along in the journey of creating an inclusive workplace:

- Diversity Awards - The Forum on Workplace Inclusion (forumworkplaceinclusion.org)
- America's Best Employers for Diversity 2021 (forbes.com)

As we've said before, most of the jobs available will be found through informal networking, but there are formal job boards which focus on underrepresented communities. Here's one: Top 25 Diversity Job Boards for More Diverse Hiring | Vervoe

Appendix B:
Additional Reading and Resources

Self-Assessment

The Myers-Briggs Type Indicator (MBTI)

www.Principlesyou.com

The Maslach Burnout Inventory, available online at mindgarden.com measures burnout on three scales: exhaustion, cynicism, and professional efficacy.

Do What You Are: Discover the Perfect Career for You Through the Secrets of Personality Type, by Paul Tieger and Barbara Barron (2021)

Job Search

The 2-Hour Job Search, by Steve Dalton, 10 Speed Press.

What Color is Your Parachute, by Richard N. Bolles with Katherine Brooks, 10 Speed Press.

Cracking the Hidden Job Market, by Donald Asher, 10 Speed Press

Pivot: The Only Move That Matters Is Your Next One. by Jenny Blake, Portfolio

The Job Search Manifesto, by Steve Hernandez and Mike Manoske, Crystal Cove Media,

Next Job, Best Job: A Headhunter's 11 Strategies to Get Hired Now, by Rob Barnett, Citadel

Switchers: How Smart Professionals Change Careers--and Seize Success Hardcover, AMACOM

Designing Your Work Life: How to Thrive and Change and Find Happiness at Work, by Bill Burnett and Dave Evans

Resume-Writing

Modernize Your Resume, by Wendy Enelow & Louise Kursmark.

Expert Resumes and Linkedin Profiles for Managers and Executives, by Wendy Enelow

How to Write a KILLER LinkedIn Profile, by Brenda Bernstein.

Job Interviewing

How to Answer Interview Questions, by Peggy McKee.

What I Wish Every Job Candidate Knew, by Russell Tuckerton.

Get That Job! The Quick and Complete Guide to a Winning Interview, by <u>Thea Kelley</u>

The Art of The Interview: The Perfect Answers To Every Interview Question By James Storey

Career Management/Engagement

The 7 Hidden Reasons Employees Leave, by F. Leigh Branham, Harper-Collins Leadership.

Re-Engage, by F. Leigh Branham and Mark D. Hirschfeld, McGraw-Hill.

HBR Guide to Your Professional Growth, Harvard Business Review Press.